GET SMART

about

TESTS

The Essential Parent and Teacher's Guide to
Understanding Children's Educational
and Psychological Testing

Joseph D. Rocchio, Ph.D.

GET SMART
about
TESTS

*The Essential Parent and Teacher's Guide to
Understanding Children's Educational
and Psychological Testing*

Joseph D. Rocchio, Ph.D.

ROCKLIN
PUBLICATIONS

To Ellen, Erin, Andrea,
and Ann.

TABLE OF CONTENTS

Chapter 3

INTRODUCTION

You're about to embark on a journey into the world of testing. It could be called the secret world of testing because most parents know very little about educational and psychological testing. They may vaguely recall taking standardized tests when they were in school, and now they see their children taking similar tests, but beyond that, most would have difficulty explaining the basic differences between an IQ test and an achievement test.

In today's world, tests are increasingly used to make important decisions about our children. That alone is enough reason to make understanding tests a top priority for all parents and teachers. Educational tests are used to decide whether a student will be held back in school, diagnosed with a learning disability, admitted to advanced classes or to a gifted program, or even allowed to graduate from high school. And the more psychologically oriented tests will help to determine if a child is experiencing depression, anxiety, impulsivity, autism, social problems, attention-deficit/hyperactivity disorder (ADHD), or any number of other conditions.

Despite the fact that tests can affect children in important ways, parents are surprisingly quiet when it comes to asking questions about tests. Parents aren't asking questions because they don't know what to ask. Parent meetings to review and explain test results occur at schools and in clinic offices all the time, but these meetings can be confusing and intimidating because a lot of technical jargon is thrown around and passed off as "discussing testing results." These meetings should be sources of useful information rather than sources of confusion.

The purpose of this book is to inform parents and teachers in an honest and straightforward manner about educational and psychological testing. Being informed means, first and foremost, appreciating that a child is more than a test score. Sometimes we get so obsessed with the numbers that we forget the importance of other aspects of a child's life. We hear things like, "Johnny's IQ is 134," or "Sally got a perfect score on the SAT!" These are legitimate reasons to celebrate, but do we take time to wonder what kind of person Johnny or Sally is beyond their scores? Do we ask, or even care, if they are motivated, curious, compassionate, generous, honest, or creative, or whether they are talented in dance, music, or mechanics?

Being informed means that parents and teachers understand the pros and cons of tests, know of acceptable alternatives to standardized testing, appreciate how tests are used to make decisions, and know how to interpret test scores. Being informed means understanding why it's important to use multiple measures—such as some combination of grades, recommendations from teachers, portfolios, and test scores—when making important decisions, rather than relying on a single test score.

And being informed means knowing how to judge whether a test is good. Tests can be useful tools, whether it's to help identify a student who needs extra help in a particular subject area or to help with making an accurate diagnosis. But the caveat here is that the tests must be good in a psychometric (technical) sense. As you will learn, this means that they must have acceptable reliability and validity. These are concepts normally buried deep inside technical manuals and generally are not discussed in much detail with the general public because they're considered to be too technical. When explained in a clear manner, though, they can be understood by just about anyone.

Because we live in a society where tests have an influential role in children's lives, there is no more important time than now to learn about tests. It's time for parents to stand up and demand better explanations and, if necessary, to challenge whether a particular test is relevant to their child's learning and school experience.

Here's a chapter-by-chapter glimpse of what to expect from *GET SMART ABOUT TESTS*:

CHAPTER 1—Welcome to the World of Testing

Do we need standardized tests? What actually is a test? And what makes a test "good?" The answers to these questions are clearly explained in this chapter. And important technical issues of reliability and validity are discussed in a reader-friendly manner (e.g., having a reliable test is like having a reliable friend). You'll also learn who can buy and administer educational and psychological tests. Lastly, with the prevalence of online IQ and personality tests, you'll learn whether these tests are useful and whether they're like the one's used in a professional's office.

CHAPTER 2—What Do All Those Numbers Mean?

Parents have a tendency to nod their heads in agreement when test scores are being discussed, even when they don't understand what's being said. This chapter will help to eliminate much of the confusion about test scores. The most common scores (e.g., standard scores, stanines, percentiles, grade-equivalents) are explained in clear, understandable language. Classification tables are included to help parents and teachers make even more sense of scores.

CHAPTER 3—Intelligence Tests

What is IQ, and is it important? This chapter answers these questions and then moves on to discuss how individuals at different IQ levels are classified. You'll also get a glimpse of how IQ tests are administered. Several important and controversial topics related to intelligence are discussed. These include: the influence that heredity and environment have on intelligence, how one's mindset can affect intelligence, whether IQ measures a person's potential, whether IQ can be boosted, and whether intelligence is better defined as a single, general ability or as multiple abilities.

CHAPTER 4—Proficiency and Achievement Tests

This chapter begins with definitions of two of the most common types of standardized tests used in schools—proficiency tests and achievement tests. This is followed by an explanation of how classifying students on the basis of their achievement test scores makes interpretation of the scores easier for parents and teachers. Alternatives to standardized tests—such as performance (authentic) assessment, portfolio assessment, and curriculum-based measurement—are also discussed.

In the wake of the *No Child Left Behind (NCLB)* legislation, proficiency testing has come under fire because of its use in high-stakes situations. This controversy is addressed, along with other important issues, such as the effects teaching to the test might have on critical thinking and on transformational mentors, whether it's a good idea to hold teachers accountable based on their students' test scores, and whether tests should be used to measure standards.

CHAPTER 5—Personality Tests

Standardized tests are not limited to IQ or proficiency/achievement tests. Personality tests are another form of standardized tests. Although they're helpful in understanding what makes us tick, they're far from being crystal balls. Chapter 5 looks at the different types of personality tests and addresses some of the major pitfalls of projective techniques such as the inkblot and draw-a-person personality tests.

CHAPTER 6—College Admissions Tests and Career Inventories

U.S. News & World Report once described the SAT as the most influential test in America. Perhaps no test receives as much media attention as the SAT. But are college admissions tests such as the SAT and ACT really needed? What would happen if colleges and universities suddenly stopped using them? Chapter 6 touches on these questions and a whole lot more, such as whether test coaching really helps or whether grade inflation—the so-called plague of education—really exists. The chapter closes with a look at how career interest inventories can be helpful when deciding on a career.

CHAPTER 7—Other Useful Tests

Several other types of tests that children are likely to encounter but were not covered in previous chapters are briefly touched upon in this chapter. These include adaptive behavior scales, visual-motor tests, behavior rating scales, neuropsychological tests, and school readiness tests. Important laws pertaining to testing that parents should become familiar with, such as *No Child Left Behind (NCLB)* and *IDEA 2004*, are covered as well.

CHAPTER 8—Helping Children Do Their Best

This chapter contains some of the most important information in this book—ways to help children do their best. It begins by looking at common obstacles to learning, such as test anxiety, self beliefs, learning disabilities, emotional disabilities, and stress. This is followed by a discussion of the many things parents can do to help their child, such as encouraging thinking and reasoning skills, using individualized instruction and interventions that work, understanding the importance of consistent school attendance, starting a support group, and reducing stress.

CHAPTER 9—Questions and Answers about Testing

Parents often have questions about testing but usually have no easy access to answers. Many real-life questions that parents have about testing are answered in this chapter. The questions cover topics such as what is underachievement, how much an independent evaluation might cost, should a child be held back in school based on test scores, what do changes in test scores mean, and much more.

APPENDIX—Commonly Used Tests

Parents and teachers are usually curious about the specific tests administered to their children and students but have not had a resource to turn to for even basic information about these tests. In the Appendix you will find a listing of over 100 tests commonly used to evaluate children. Information on each test includes: name of test, publisher, type of test (e.g., individually administered, self-report), what it's used for (e.g., to assess emotional functioning, to assess level of intellectual functioning), the age range for which it is used, and the time it takes to administer the test.

What you will not find in this book is an indictment of standardized testing. *Good* tests that are *properly* used serve an important purpose when combined with other information about a child. Abandoning the use of standardized testing would leave us with the undesirable alternative of allowing personal opinion, biases, prejudices, or fortuitous circumstances to enter the assessment process and guide decision-making. But an important caution is in order, and that is, even good tests can be harmful if used improperly. That's why it is so important to be informed.

GET SMART ABOUT TESTS is written specifically for parents and teachers, but because testing permeates virtually all aspects of society, it is likely to be of considerable interest to others as well. This would include school counselors, education administrators, college students planning a career in counseling or psychology or education, mental health professionals, pediatricians, family physicians, education reporters, judges, attorneys, education policymakers, legislators, or for that matter, anyone interested in an honest perspective on educational and psychological testing.

Because of the vastness of the field of testing (volumes upon volumes of academic textbooks have been written on this subject), it is impossible to cover all aspects of testing or to provide details of the hundreds of published tests in such a short book. What this book will do is touch on some of the most common uses and most important issues related to children and testing. It is hoped that you will develop a basic yet solid understanding of educational and psychological testing, and ultimately, will become a smarter consumer of tests.

CHAPTER 1

Welcome to the World of Testing

It's easy to imagine a time when standardized tests will be used across every segment of society, from preschool through high school and into college; for local, state, and federal jobs; for firefighters, police officers, barbers and cosmetologists, electricians, plumbers, teachers, psychologists, lawyers, and physicians; the list is almost endless. It's easy to imagine because we live in that society now.

Nearly all of the 50 million school-age children in the United States will be exposed to some form of standardized testing during the course of their education. Preschool children will take readiness tests. Elementary school, middle school, and high school students will take proficiency tests. And many of those same high school students also will have to face the challenge of college admissions tests. Add to those numbers all the children evaluated in hospital clinics, mental health centers, and private clinics who will be administered IQ tests, personality tests, achievement tests, visual-motor tests, and a whole array of other standardized tests.

In all these instances, tests will be used to make some type of decision about children, with the potential to influence their futures in dramatic ways. And even after high school, tests will be lurking somewhere, usually as gatekeepers to college, or to medical, dental, law, or graduate school. They also will be used to determine one's suitability for a job or promotion. Tests are everywhere, and they are impossible to avoid. We truly have become a testing society. In fact, never before have standardized tests been used as much as they are today.

Do We Need Standardized Tests?

What would happen if we didn't have standardized tests? Society probably would look much as it does now. Amazing scientific discoveries would continue to be made. Great works of art and grand musical compositions would still be created. And we as a society would not perish. Why, then, should we use standardized tests?

Without standardized tests, society has the potential of being a minefield filled with personal impressions, biases, and prejudices whenever someone makes a decision about us. Tests can help to clean up that minefield.

Imagine what it would be like if getting a job, being promoted, or getting into college depended on our physical appearance or on whether we had a friend or family member making the decision. Using well-designed objective tests makes the decision-making process fairer. That's because objective tests, such as true/false and multiple-choice tests, are scored according to standard procedures, so no matter who scores the test and regardless of the scorer's biases and prejudices, the results will be the same.

It's important to understand, though, that using standardized tests merely reduces the influences that prejudices and other biases can have on a decision; it does not eliminate them. And it reduces these negative influences only if the test is designed to be fair and is used in a fair manner. Otherwise, even objective tests could favor a specific group of individuals and give them an unfair advantage.

Not only does standardized testing contribute to a fairer society, it also makes for a more efficient one in terms of time and money. It's far easier and far more cost efficient, for example, for a college to use the results from standardized tests, such as the SAT or ACT, to screen thousands of applicants than it is to interview each applicant individually. The same is true for the military and business worlds where tests streamline the process of determining the aptitudes and interests for large numbers of people.

The benefits of standardized testing go beyond the broad areas of fairness and efficiency. Standardized tests are also used routinely to evaluate a child's academic strengths and weaknesses, to identify unknown talents or abilities, to help make accurate clinical and educational diagnoses, to determine if educational standards are being met, and to answer the most fundamental question that parents have, which is, "Is my child learning?"

It's Not All Good News

Because of benefits like these, standardized tests have become an accepted and basically unchallenged aspect of the American educational landscape. Hidden among the benefits, though, is a rarely discussed aspect of tests—they can be wrong. For example, a test might show that a child has attention-deficit/hyperactivity disorder (ADHD) when the child does not, or it may indicate that a child does not have ADHD when he or she actually does. These types of mistakes or errors are called *false positives* and *false negatives*. False positives occur when a test says a problem *is* present when in fact it is not. False negatives occur when a test says a problem is *not* present when in fact it is. These errors occur in *all* tests. In other words, no test is perfect.

Despite the fact that tests are not perfect, educators and psychologists sometimes operate as though they are. We see this in the way schools use strict cutoff scores with graduation tests and proficiency tests, where even one point can keep a student from graduating or from meeting an academic standard. It's understandable why schools do this. Test experts use a lot of statistical formulas and scientific-sounding terms when developing tests of intelligence or achievement, or any test for that matter. This gives the impression, though false, that these tests are as precise as scientific instruments. On top of that is the fact that we're mentally primed from an early age to think in terms of exact numbers. We understand, for example, that there are 12 eggs in a dozen, that the length of a football field is 100 yards, that our body temperature is 98.6 degrees Fahrenheit, or that the speed limit on the open highway is 65 miles per hour. So it makes sense that we have come to expect the same exactness with tests.

The problem, though, is that educational and psychological tests are not as accurate as precision scientific instruments. Our dynamic inner world of thoughts and feelings, as well as complex concepts such as intelligence and school achievement, cannot be measured as precisely as our physical world. As sophisticated as tests are, they cannot explain the uniqueness of a child with complete accuracy. With this in mind, we need to think of test scores as good *estimates* rather than as precise or exact measures.

Society's Reverence for Tests

As we saw in the previous section, educators and psychologists sometimes treat tests as perfect measures of a child's performance, completely free of bias or error. And society in general also tends to view tests as foolproof. Consider an editorial in a major metropolitan newspaper in which it was proposed that prospective judges be required to take a standardized test as a condition of running for judicial office. (This came after a Common Pleas judge issued an opinion the editorial board of the paper strongly disagreed with.) This idea is driven by the belief that a standardized test would be able to accurately identify competent judicial candidates so that no matter who wins, the public can at least be assured that the person elected will be competent.

Such an idea reflects a naiveté about tests, even among bright and supposedly well-informed individuals, and it contributes to an undeserved reverence for tests. The flaw in this reasoning is readily exposed by the fact that society already requires most professionals (including attorneys who eventually become judges) to take rigorous standardized exams before being allowed to offer services to the public. Despite that, every professional group will have members who are incompetent. That's because passing a standardized test does not make one competent. Humans are too complex for tests to accurately predict how they'll perform in every situation they encounter.

This reverence toward tests is particularly evident in our schools. At one middle school, an eighth-grade girl and her parents met with a school counselor to plan her high school courses. Although she was taking an advanced math course and doing very well, the counselor said it was "school policy" for students who do not score high enough on the math section of the state-mandated proficiency test to take an "intervention" math course, regardless of past math grades.

At an elementary school, a mother was told that her son probably would not be able to continue in the school's reading enrichment program the following year because his proficiency test scores in reading were not high enough, despite being an excellent reader and having an A in the class. Although proficiency test scores are part of the admission criteria for the class, it makes no sense to give tests greater importance than actual classroom performance.

And many states now require students to pass a graduation test in order to receive a diploma. Regardless of a student's grade point average (GPA) or past academic accomplishments, passing the test is considered to be the ultimate proof that his or her education is legitimate.

These are examples of what psychologists refer to as *making the predictor (the test) more important than the criteria (real-life events)*. This practice is widespread, and it's perpetuated by the belief that tests are better predictors than real-life performance. A better way to make decisions is to consider real-life performance along with test scores. Real-life performance includes things like grades, teacher recommendations, past academic accomplishments, portfolios, and even past test scores. Looking at several factors rather a single test score increases the chances of making the best decision.

Now, let's turn our attention to the definition of tests. Most of you already have a good idea what a test is. After all, you had to take tests when you were in school. What you will find here, though, is a more detailed definition that will give you a much clearer picture of tests.

What Is A Test?

What image comes to mind when you think of tests? Is it a quiet classroom with rows of students at their desks, pencils in hand and heads bowed, taking a classroom test as the teacher slowly walks the aisles casting eagle-eye glances from left to right? Is it the joy in a daughter's face when she learns that she got into a gifted class because of her high score on an IQ test, or the anguish in a dejected son's face after learning that he did not get into the college his heart was set on because of average SAT or ACT scores? Or maybe it's simply remembering the fear and nervousness over the driving test you took many years ago.

Although our images of tests may differ, most people seem to agree that they stir up a lot of anxiety. In fact, the mere thought of taking a test can turn even the most confident among us into nervous wrecks. Often the anxiety is based on a fear—a fear that the test will not fairly tap our skills or abilities, or that it somehow will be used to keep us from reaching a long-desired goal. But others view tests in a much more positive light—as necessary gatekeepers that impartially separate the smart from the not so smart, the competent from the incompetent, or the emotionally fit from the psychologically troubled.

So what exactly is this thing called a test, this thing that is sometimes revered and other times feared? Here's a good basic definition: *A test is a set of standard procedures for measuring a sampling, or part, of a person's behaviors in an objective manner.*

This is a definition of a *standardized* test. IQ tests, achievement and proficiency tests, and true/false personality tests are all examples of standardized tests. Standardized tests use *standard* procedures, meaning they are administered and scored according to a standard set of rules, whether the person lives in California or Ohio or Texas. The same questions are asked in the same manner, the same areas are covered, and the same scoring procedures are used.

Besides using standard procedures, another feature of tests is that they measure only a *sampling,* or part, of a person's total behaviors. Why only a sampling? Because it would be impractical to measure every single skill or behavior a person possesses. Using a test is more efficient because it measures a small portion (a sampling) of skills or behaviors. In other words, *tests are shortcuts to learning about people.*

Another important characteristic of standardized tests is that they are *objective.* An example of an objective test is a true/false test, or a multiple-choice test, like the kind you took when you got your driver's license. With objective tests, no matter who scores the test, the results should be the same. The examiner or scorer's beliefs, values, prejudices, thoughts, or feelings about a person do not affect the results. These beliefs, prejudices, and so on are called *biases.* It's important to reduce these biases as much as possible because they can lead to discrimination and unfair treatment. Reducing bias is a major advantage of objective tests over other types of tests.

Although objective scoring procedures reduce bias and make tests fairer, they do not eliminate bias. It's impossible to completely eliminate bias from tests because people make up the questions on objective true/false or multiple-choice tests. People by nature are *subjective* and tend to see things from their own point of view and can unintentionally inject their views into test questions.

Kinds of Tests

The standardized tests children will be required to take over the course of their education can be narrowed down to two basic types: 1) tests that compare a student's scores to the scores of other children (called *norm-based tests*), and 2) tests that compare their scores to a target or goal (called *criterion-referenced tests*). Both types are widely used in schools and in clinics across the country, and both have important roles.

Tests That Compare Your Child to Others (Norm-referenced Tests)

Most of the standardized tests a child will encounter will be *norm-referenced* tests. Norm-referenced tests, as the name implies, use norms. A *norm* is simply the average or "normal" performance of a group of children on a certain test. When a child takes a norm-referenced test, he or she is compared to similar children in this norm group. Norm-referenced tests answer the question, "How is my child doing in comparison to his or her classmates?" By using norms we are able to determine if the child is above average, average, or below average, compared to similar children. Examples of norm-referenced tests are IQ tests, achievement tests, and proficiency tests.

Norm-referenced tests are commonly used to *classify* students; therefore, these tests are often used to evaluate students for gifted programs or other special education programs. As noted, they're used whenever you want to compare a child's performance to other children of the same age or grade.

The content areas covered by norm-referenced tests tend to be broad. For that reason, what the test measures may not be the same as what students have been taught in the classroom. When this mismatch between test content and classroom curriculum occurs, educators say that the test is "poorly aligned." Understandably, this has been a major criticism of using norm-referenced achievement tests with high-stakes decisions. It doesn't make sense, not to mention it's unfair, to test children on material they've never been exposed to in the classroom.

Tests That Compare Your Child's Score to a Goal (Criterion-reference Tests)

The other type of test your child will encounter is called a *criterion-referenced* test. Criterion-referenced tests go by different names, such as *content-referenced tests* or *objective-referenced tests,* but *criterion-referenced* is by far the term most commonly used.

The main difference between criterion-referenced tests and norm-referenced tests is that criterion-referenced tests *do not* use norms. So, instead of answering the question, "How is this student doing in comparison to his or her classmates?" as is the case with norm-referenced tests, criterion-reference tests answer the question, "What can this student do?" in subjects such as math, spelling, or science.

Criterion-referenced tests are used when students are expected to reach a specific target or goal called the *criterion*. For example, the target or goal might be that all students in a math class will be expected to subtract 50 three-digit numbers with 90% accuracy. (In other words, they must get at least 45 out of the 50 problems correct in order to meet the goal.) Another example of a criterion-referenced test is a driver's license test. With this test, a person must correctly answer a specified number of questions correctly (the goal) before being issued a license, no matter how others have done on the test.

Criterion-referenced tests can be particularly useful because they are highly individualized. They can help determine a child's specific academic strengths and weaknesses, which are then used to develop tailor-made instructional strategies. In other words, these tests tell us if a child has mastered a particular set of skills and, if not, where instruction should be targeted.

Another plus of criterion-referenced tests is that the areas covered on the test are the same areas being taught in the classroom. For that reason, some experts consider these tests to be more appropriate than norm-referenced tests for measuring progress in school and for helping to make high-stakes decisions.

What Is a "Good" Test?

To the average person, it's easy to think of all tests as being good, sometimes for no other reason than because we're told they're good or because they're colorfully and professionally packaged and skillfully marketed. Although test specialists put a lot of hard work and great care into making sure the tests they develop are good enough to be used in making decisions about people, that doesn't mean all tests are created equal. In fact, some tests *are* better than others.

But how can you tell if a test is good? The most surefire way is by asking the right questions. And in order to ask the right questions, you first must have a fundamental understanding of some basic testing concepts. The most important concepts are *reliability* and *validity*. Although these are technical concepts, as you will see they can be fairly easy to understand.

A Good Test Is Reliable, Like a Good Friend

A good way to understand the concept of reliability is to think of a person in your life, perhaps a good friend, whom you consider to be reliable. When you think of this person, what comes to mind? Is he or she someone you can count on or *depend* on most of the time? Is he or she someone you can *rely* on? Probably. In other words, good friends are dependable and reliable in most situations. Of course, your friend may be late from time to time because of heavy traffic, weather conditions, or an accident, or maybe she simply lost track of time. Like good tests, good friends are not perfect, but they still can be good friends.

Reliability is a desirable quality in a friend, and it's also a desirable quality in a test. A reliable test means that you can depend on a child's test score being *approximately* the same (not necessarily exactly the same) if he or she were tested again with the same test or with an equivalent form of the test.

Let's use an IQ test as an example, but remember, reliability applies to *all* standardized tests. On a reliable IQ test, a child who received an IQ of 130 when he or she was first tested likely will get a similar but slightly different score if tested a second time with the same or similar version of the test. The second score may be 126, 127, 128, 129, 131, 132, 133, or 134. It's expected to be somewhere in the neighborhood of 130, but not necessarily exactly 130. In fact, it would be unusual for a child to get the same score on a retest, even on a very reliable test. It does happen, but not too often.

Why the difference between the first and second scores? It's that pesky thing called *measurement error* (technically known as the *standard error of measurement*). Measurement error is always a part of test scores. But that's OK as long as the error is not too great. Small differences in scores are expected in reliable tests; big differences are not. In other words, scores on standardized tests do change, and they're actually expected to change, but not by too much if the test is reliable.

If a child's test and retest IQ scores are extremely different, for example, a 130 on the first testing and a 109 on the second, something obviously is causing this. The test may not be reliable, or perhaps the child was not trying her best the second time because of a "Who cares?" attitude, or maybe she was ill with the flu or developed a serious medical problem that interfered with her mental performance. Maybe she was preoccupied with family problems, or maybe other stresses in her life caused her to be distracted. Life is complicated and often stressful even for children, and so many things can affect test scores. Table 1 lists some of those things:

Table 1

Some Things That Can Affect Test Performance

Anxiety	Poor night's rest	Motivation
Depression	Interests	Fears/worries
Attitude	Mental illness	Poor attention
Stomachache	Vision problems	Headache
Hearing problems	Physical illness	Hunger
Problems with friends	Family problems	Fear of failure
Recent argument	Lack of persistence	Fatigue
Low self-esteem	Lack of self-confidence	Self beliefs

Reliability is important because we want to be able to "rely" on the test scores when we make decisions. Reliability typically does not apply to classroom tests, however. Consider the example of a child who fails a classroom spelling test on Monday but is permitted to retake it on Wednesday. If he decides to skip his after-school TV programs on Monday and Tuesday in order to study his spelling words an extra half-hour each day, it's possible that he could get an A on the same test he failed on Monday!

Dramatic changes like this are expected to occur with classroom tests because *immediate, active learning* is taking place in the here and now. In other words, classroom tests measure short-term learning. In contrast, standardized achievement tests, such as proficiency tests, usually are designed to measure *long-term learning*. They measure the accumulation of *all* the classroom learning (often years of learning), and the results are expected to be more stable (reliable) over time.

It's Important to Have
Confidence in Test Scores

It should be apparent by now that test scores are not perfect. Many people, though, still believe that concepts such as intelligence and achievement, or personality traits, can be measured with the same precision that we're able to measure physical characteristics, such as height or weight. We've become accustomed to think of a test score as exact and unchanging. In reality, it's neither.

Many psychologists, when reporting test scores, use *confidence intervals* (sometimes called *confidence bands*) alongside the scores. This is done to alert you to the fact that the scores are not perfect and can change slightly. *Confidence intervals are ranges of scores that tell you where a person's "true score" probably falls.* In a perfect world, a person's "true score" is an absolutely accurate measure of their abilities or skills. Of course, this isn't a perfect world, so we can only provide a reasonably good estimate of where their "true score" falls, which is somewhere between the scores of the confidence interval.

Let's look at an IQ score as an example. If a student receives an IQ of 127, the confidence interval that goes with this score might look something like this in a report.

		(95% Confidence Interval)
IQ..................127		122–132

The confidence interval simply gives you an idea how confident you can be in a score. In this example, you can be 95% confident that this student's "true IQ" falls somewhere between 122 and 132. That's a fairly high level of confidence. Another common confidence interval is 90%, which means that you can be 90% confident that a person's "true IQ" falls within a certain range of scores.

Confidence intervals are used with scores on many types of standardized tests, such as IQ tests and achievement/proficiency tests. Using confidence intervals is a better way of reporting scores than simply reporting a score by itself. Again, the reason is that the confidence interval lets you know that scores are not perfect and could change somewhat.

A Good Test Must Be Accurate, Too

Test reliability is important, but validity is considered by some experts to be the most important aspect of tests. *A valid test is a test that accurately measures what it was designed to measure.* The math portion of a proficiency test, for example, should measure math skills only, not reading skills or spelling skills or any other skill—just math skills. Likewise, a valid intelligence test should measure intelligence, and a valid musical aptitude test should measure musical aptitude.

In order to understand validity, it might be helpful to think back to when you were in elementary school. Maybe you had a teacher who would give spelling tests and take off points for poor handwriting. You might have spelled all the words correctly but still didn't get an "A."

This technically would not be a valid or "good" test of spelling because you also have to be a neat writer. Picture the student who spelled all the words correctly but got an F because of poor (but legible) handwriting, and another student with neat handwriting who misspelled four words and got a B. A good spelling test should measure spelling only; a good writing test should measure writing only; and so on. That is what a valid test is supposed to do—measure what it was designed to measure.

Validity, of course, is not limited to classroom tests. *All* tests should be valid. But this is particularly true for standardized tests because they're often used to make important decisions.

Sometimes standardized tests are used improperly when they are used for purposes other than for which they were designed. For example, a college admissions test specifically designed to predict high school students' success in their first year of college would not be valid for predicting high school students' success in an advanced language program. If it's to be used for that purpose, then it should be demonstrated that it's valid for that purpose.

Good validity is the hallmark of a good test, and it is a concept that every parent and educator should be familiar with. A test with no proven validity is useless because you can never be sure what the test is actually measuring.

Tests, Tests Everywhere!

Testing is a huge business. Hundreds of educational and psychological tests are on the market today. These tests cover just about every facet of human behavior you can imagine, ranging from reading and arithmetic, to musical and mechanical aptitude, to depression and anxiety, to parenting satisfaction and parenting stress.

Table 2 will give you some idea of what the different types of tests used by psychologists and other testing professionals measure.

Table 2

A Sample of What Tests Measure

Intelligence	Mathematics	Personality types
Reading recognition	Reading comprehension	Visual-motor skills
Self-esteem	Eating disorders	Depression
Career interests	Anxiety	Hopelessness
Independent living	Parenting satisfaction	Parenting stress
Personnel selection	Learning disabilities	Substance abuse
Memory	Behavior problems	Autism
Infant development	Asperger's disorder	Stress
Motor skills	Learning styles	Leadership
Mechanical aptitude	Musical aptitude	Auditory learning
School readiness	Speech & language	Alcohol use
Attention deficit	Sleep disorders	Critical thinking
Verbal learning	Temperament	Hyperactivity
Eating attitudes	Emotional intelligence	Marital satisfaction

Companies that publish tests sell millions of standardized educational and psychological tests each year to professionals employed by school systems, private and governmental agencies, businesses, hospitals, clinics, and professionals in private practice. The use of tests is spread across all segments of society, but students—those from kindergarten through college—form the largest segment.

Who Can Administer Educational and Psychological Tests?

Standardized educational and psychological tests are sophisticated instruments. Years of work usually go into developing a good test. As a consumer, you will see only the final product—the test booklet in front of you, or in front of your child or student.

The professionals who administer standardized educational and psychological tests often are psychologists, but other professionals, such as counselors or vocational and educational specialists, as well as classroom teachers, are permitted to administer some tests. The classroom teacher, for example, typically will be the one who administers the proficiency tests your child will take in school. (Most tests administered by teachers, such as quizzes and classroom tests, are developed by the teachers themselves and are a different breed than the standardized educational and psychological tests that take years to develop.) A career or vocational counselor may give career interest inventories and certain aptitude tests in order to help a student choose the right career path. And an educational specialist may administer certain educational tests to determine whether a learning problem exists or to determine which remedial approach works best for a particular student.

Because standardized educational and psychological tests are sophisticated instruments, anyone who administers them must be properly trained *and* have experience administering and interpreting tests. This is important because the person using the tests needs to be familiar with the tests' technical and statistical properties to make sure they are the right tests for the child being evaluated. Just as it would be unwise to have an untrained and inexperienced person perform and interpret medical tests, it would be equally unwise, and unethical, to have an untrained and inexperienced person administer and interpret educational or psychological tests.

The psychologists, educational specialists, and counseling professionals who administer tests are highly trained. Many will have a doctoral degree—a Ph.D. (Doctor of Philosophy), a Psy.D. (Doctor of Psychology), or an Ed.D. (Doctor of Education)—but a good many also will have a specialist degree, such as an Ed.S. (Educational Specialist), or a master's degree, such as an M.A. (Master of Arts), an M.S. (Master of Science), or an M.Ed. (Master of

Education). You may be wondering whether medical doctors, such as M.D.s (Doctor of Medicine) and D.O.s (Doctor of Osteopathy) administer tests psychological or educational tests. Typically they do not.

Having one of the above degrees does not necessarily mean a person is qualified to administer and interpret psychological and educational tests. They also must be licensed or certified through state licensing boards (or be supervised by someone who is licensed or certified). And in order to become licensed or certified, they must have appropriate training and experience in addition to passing a rigorous written exam and oftentimes an oral exam.

Who Can Buy Educational and Psychological Tests?

Educational and psychological tests also cannot be purchased by just anyone. As explained in the previous section, companies that publish tests have specific qualifications for *users* of tests, and similar qualifications extend to the *purchasers* of tests. These qualifications usually require a college degree (typically a master's or doctoral degree) and proper training and experience in educational and psychological testing.

Restricting the use and sale of tests to qualified individuals is done to protect the public. Imagine what it would be like if educational and psychological tests could be purchased at the local bookstore. People might try to determine whether they, their son or daughter, or a friend has a learning disability or an emotional problem. Such self-diagnosis would be replete with serious risks. For one, a genuine problem could be missed, with the potential for tragic consequences. Or one might conclude that a problem exists when it doesn't, creating unnecessary anxiety.

Limiting the purchase of tests to professionals also prevents the tests from becoming useless. It's tempting to want to know in advance what questions are going to be on a test, especially if it gives us an advantage, such as securing a competitive job or getting into a highly selective college. But if tests and the answers to the test questions were widely available to anyone, they quickly would lose their ability to give accurate results. And test publishers would constantly have to create new tests, which is no easy feat when considering that it often takes years to produce a good test.

Using Computers in Testing

With the widespread use of computers these days, it should come as no surprise that computers play an important role in educational and psychological testing. Although traditional paper-and-pencil tests are still common, an appealing option now exists—having individuals answer test questions directly from a computer. This is usually done in an office or school setting where a professional staff is available to answer questions and to make sure the conditions will lead to a valid testing.

Scoring has been the most common use of computers in educational and psychological testing, but computers also are increasingly being used for the more complex task of test interpretation. In fact, in schools, clinics, and private practices across the country, psychologists and other testing professionals now routinely use interpretive software for a wide range of tests, including some of the most popular intelligence, achievement, and personality tests.

Computerized testing has a number of advantages. Among the most obvious is fast scoring, which makes the results available almost immediately. Butcher, Perry, and Hahn (2004) also reported that computerized personality testing tends to produce more comprehensive reports, is more objective, and is more reliable than testing conducted by a person.

Perhaps most important, though, has to do with the accuracy in making predictions. For example, Butcher and his colleagues report that predictions from computerized testings that utilize statistical rules tend to be more accurate than predictions based on a professional clinician's judgment. In other words, computerized personality testing stacks up quite well against the more traditional clinician-based testing, and in some instances may even be better.

Can You Place Faith in Online Testing?

Computerized testing of the kind we've been talking about can be an important part of the evaluation process, and it usually takes place under the watchful eye of a professional who has appropriate training and experience and who is guided by the ethical standards of their profession. But what about another kind of computerized testing, such as the kind found on the Internet? Are these tests the same as those a professional would administer in the office or school? Is the information these tests provide useful?

The number of online tests available to anyone with access to the Internet is huge. Areas covered include IQ, personality, career exploration, anxiety and depression screening, ADHD screening, self-esteem, assertiveness, relationships, leadership, temperament, emotional IQ, communication skills, and much more.

People are instinctively curious creatures, and this curiosity has contributed to the popularity of these online tests. But if you've ever wondered whether these are the same tests that psychologists and other testing professionals use, the answer is no. An online IQ test, for example, is very different from the type of IQ test that is administered in a professional's office or in a school setting. In fact, most testing Web sites post a disclaimer stating that the tests on their sites are for entertainment purposes only and not for professional use. It is highly unlikely that a school system, agency, or professional would seriously consider the results from online tests to be acceptable for any type of decision making.

Some Web sites, though, do offer online versions of the traditional, professionally developed paper-and-pencil tests that are used in clinics or private practices. These online versions are available only to qualified professionals who purchase the tests for use with their clients, who take them online. And some Web sites sponsored by institutions, such as hospitals, offer seemingly useful screening tests for problems such as depression and anxiety. These tests, too, usually have a disclaimer informing the consumer that the results are not intended as a substitute for face-to-face professional consultation.

An objection to many online tests is that no technical data are readily available, if at all, to evaluate the usefulness of the tests. And even if such data were available, the average person is not likely to have the technical expertise to understand the data.

Another particularly important concern is related to supervision. Online tests are usually taken in the privacy of one's home, so professional oversight of the test taker is nonexistent. Compare this to a school, clinic, or private practice setting where professionals are readily available if problems arise. A person who reacts adversely to the results of an online test could be psychologically out on a limb without a safety net. For example, a low score on an online IQ test could wreak havoc on a person suffering from depression or someone plagued with low self-esteem. Rather than placing blind faith in these tests, prospective users should make a point to thoroughly read the information on the test's Web site, including all the fine print and any disclaimers, before deciding if the test is useful to them.

The Role of Culture in Testing

Culture can be defined as the belief systems, attitudes, values, knowledge, and experiences shared by a group of people that distinguishes that group from other groups. Culture is a bond that connects people. We see this in the ethnic neighborhoods scattered across the United States where churches, schools, markets, and social organization are centered around specific immigrant groups. Culture is consider so important as it relates to understanding human behavior that it's discussed in just about every psychology textbook in colleges across America.

The importance of culture in testing cannot be overstated. We have a history in this country of using tests inappropriately with people of different cultures. Among the most famous examples of abuse occurred during the early 1900s when immigrants at Ellis Island had to hurdle mental tests, despite not understanding English well enough to respond appropriately. These abuses were not intentional but were based on ignorance about cultural differences. We've learned a lot over the years, and ignorance can no longer be used as an excuse for discrimination.

Just how culturally diverse are our nation's schools? According to an Urban Institute's analysis of Census Bureau data, 27% of U.S. school-age children whose parents are immigrants were born in their native countries, such as Mexico, Asia, Latin America, and European countries (Capps et al., 2005). For the sake of fairness and accuracy, educational and psychological tests must be used in a manner that accommodates this diversity.

According to test experts Cohen and Swerdlik (2005), when working with persons from diverse cultures, one of the most important questions examiners should ask when choosing a test is how fair the test is with members of that culture. (Parents and teachers should be thinking along these same lines when reviewing testing result of their culturally diverse child or student.) Why is culture important? Because persons of different cultures may read a test question and understand it differently from those in the mainstream culture. This could lead to skewed or inaccurate results. People from different cultures often interpret their life experiences based on their belief systems, values, personal and cultural identities, and overall acculturation to the broader culture. What may be a taboo in one culture may be a custom in another, or what may be abnormal behavior to one person may be quite normal to a person of a different culture.

Schools are well aware of the role of culture in testing and understand that it's their responsibility to make sure all children are evaluated fairly. This means that evaluations must be conducted in a way that is racially or culturally nondiscriminatory and in the child's native language. If needed, other modes of communication (e.g., sign language) must be provided to ensure fairness and accuracy. In general, because schools are under the watchful eye of the federal government, they seem to do a reasonably good job of testing culturally diverse students.

When concerns about testing or any educational matter arise, parents must be willing to ask questions and, if necessary, to challenge a decision. But schools can be intimidating places to parents who are new to this country. Parents may feel uncomfortable or even frightened about asking questions, whether it's about testing or any matter. They may lack confidence in their English-speaking skills or may not speak English at all. Consequently, they may be inclined to shy away from asking questions or from going to their child's school altogether.

In these situations, the parent may want to ask a relative, or perhaps a neighbor or friend who speaks their language, to accompany them to the school. Local parent groups or community groups organized around their particular culture may be able to offer guidance. If going to school is just too scary a prospect, consider having an interpreter write a letter expressing your concerns to the school psychologist, counselor, principal, or teacher. Most school personnel will do their best to answer parents' questions.

Now that you have a fundamental understanding of tests, the next step is to learn about the different types of test scores. Knowing how to decode the various scores and how to make sense of the confusing jargon used to explain them will help to reduce the mystique of tests.

CHAPTER 2

What Do All Those Numbers Mean?

It's almost time for the parent-teacher conference. You drive up to the school, park the car, and amble along the walkway, through the double doors and down the hallway to your child's classroom. You casually glance inside the classroom and see the teacher and a parent getting up from their seats, talking, smiling, and shaking hands. Soon it will be your turn. Your stomach begins to churn and suddenly you find yourself becoming a bit tense. After all, the teacher will be going over your child's classroom progress and recent test results.

To some parents, an experience like this can be nerve-racking and even intimidating. Although it may be hard to eliminate all the nervousness you might be feeling, such an experience does not have to be intimidating. Being informed about test scores will help you develop a clearer understanding of your child's strengths and weaknesses, and it can increase your confidence when it comes to talking about test results with your child's teacher. Also, aside from surprising your child's teacher or counselor with your newfound knowledge of tests and scores, you are less likely to be brushed aside when asking questions.

For teachers, you are likely to feel more confident in your ability to speak knowledgably about scores not only with parents, but with psychologists, colleagues, and administrators as well. Most important, though, is that both parents and teachers will be able to make better decisions about their children and students.

The most confusing aspects of test are the scores, and there are a lot of them. You will see things such as "national percentile rank," "local percentile rank," "standard score," "stanine," "grade equivalent," "age equivalent," and more. Before getting into the meanings of the different scores, let's first discuss some of the things you should do when you get a copy of an educational or psychological report.

What to Do When You Get the Test Results

Stories of how tests have been misused or used unfairly are routinely seen in magazines and newspapers. In fact, entire books have been written criticizing standardized testing. This barrage of negative publicity has caused some parents to believe that standardized tests are worthless. But what if the results actually do provide accurate information about your child? Rather than risk dismissing useful information, it's better to first thoroughly understand what the results mean so that you can make an informed decision as to whether they accurately represent your child's performance.

Standardized test scores are reported to parents in two basic ways. The most common way is for parents to receive a computer-generated report from the school, usually a month or so after students have taken group proficiency tests. The other way is when the child is evaluated individually, which could be by a psychologist affiliated with the school system, a psychologist in private practice, or another testing professional such as an educational specialist. In these situations, parents usually receive a copy of their child's results in the form of a more personalized report, which could be a few pages to several pages in length.

Whichever report you receive, as you read through it write down any questions you have. Schedule an appointment with your child's teacher, school counselor, principal, or school psychologist to go over your questions. If your child was evaluated individually by a school psychologist, a private psychologist, or another testing professional, the results should have been thoroughly explained to you in person. If not, or if you have questions at a later time, get in touch with the person who did the evaluation to have your questions answered.

Parents do not have to feel frustrated, ashamed, or intimidated because they do not know how to make sense of test scores. They do not have to nod their heads in agreement, acting as if they understand what's being said out of a fear of appearing unintelligent. Parents should ask questions when they're uncertain about something and continue to ask questions until they have a reasonable understanding of what the results mean. Nothing should keep a parent from understanding important information about their child.

The Scores

Let's look at some of the scores parents and teachers are most likely to come across. These include:

1. Raw score
2. Standard score
3. Stanine
4. T-score
5. Scaled score
6. Percentile
7. Grade equivalent
8. Age equivalent

Although not nearly as common, you also may encounter three other types of test scores. These include:

1. Standard age score
2. Normal curve equivalent
3. Zone of proximal development

Each of these will be discussed briefly. It's not necessary to know every technical detail about these scores, but it is important for you to be somewhat familiar with them because they're so often used in educational and psychological reports.

Raw Score

The raw score is the most basic score in a test report, and it's the easiest to understand. A raw score is simply the number of questions a student answers correctly. In many standardized testing reports, this might be in a column labeled "raw scores," "number answered correctly," or something similar.

As far as a child's performance is concerned, raw scores on most tests provide little useful information. Yes, you'll be able to see that your son or daughter, let's say, correctly answered 15 of 20 questions, but you won't know how their performance compares to that of other children. But once raw scores are statistically prepared, they are transformed into useful scores like the standard scores and percentiles described below.

Standard Score

Many parents and educators are familiar with scores such as percentiles or grade equivalents, which will be discussed in a moment, but surprisingly few have an adequate understanding of standard scores, despite their widespread use. Standard scores are among the most meaningful and useful types of scores from both a practical and technical point of view, so they tend to be a favorite of psychologists.

Where will you see standard scores? On IQ tests (an IQ is a standard score), on school achievement and proficiency tests, and on many other tests. In fact, virtually all standardized tests use some type of standard score. For that reason, it's a good idea to know about this type of score.

An important characteristic of standard scores is that they're "normally distributed." This means that if we were to look at the test scores of, let's say, 1000 students, the distribution of scores would take the shape of a bell, or what some call a bell curve. In a bell curve, most of the scores fall in the middle (average range) and fewer scores fall toward the ends (the below average and above average ranges). Many things in life are normally distributed and have a bell shape, such as height, weight, and IQ.

So, what is a standard score? In its simplest form, a standard score tells us how far a person's test score is from average. For example, if a student received a raw score of 47 on a test, we would know very little about how this student actually performed compared to other students of the same age or grade. But by converting the raw score into a standard score, we would be able to tell if the student scored above average, average, or below average—compared to other children.

The standard scores used on IQ and achievement tests will have a mean (average) of 100 and a standard deviation of 15 (sometimes 16). The standard deviation will be discussed in detail later, but for now you can think of it as the degree to which test scores are spread out.

Table 3 shows a typical standard score classification system used with most IQ and achievement tests. You won't need to memorize this system because whenever standard scores are reported to parents or teachers, they usually are accompanied with their classification. So, if a student receives a standard score of 124 on an IQ test, it will be reported that this score falls in the Superior range (or some similarly named classification).

Table 3

Typical Standard Score Classification System
for IQ and Achievement Tests

Standard Score	Classification
130 and higher	Very Superior
120-129	Superior
110-119	High Average
90-109	Average
80-89	Low Average
70-79	Borderline
69 and lower	Significantly Below Average

Stanine

Another type of standard score often seen in testing reports is the *stanine* (pronounced "stay-nine"). Stanines range from 1 to 9 and have a mean (average) of 5 and a standard deviation of 2.

Stanines are easy to interpret because there are only nine stanine scores. The stanine classification system presented in Table 4 gives you an idea of its simplicity, which is what makes it so appealing.

Table 4

A Stanine Classification System

Stanine	Classification
9	Very High
7, 8	Above Average
4, 5, 6	Average
2, 3	Below Average
1	Very Low

Although stanines provide basically the same information as other standard scores, they do so with less precision. For example, only three stanine scores (4, 5, 6) cover the average range in the above classification. Compare this to the 20 scores (90 through 109) that are in the average range of a typical standard score classification system like the one discussed earlier.

T-score

The *T-score* is a type of standard score typically used with personality tests and behavioral checklists, but they can be found on other types of tests as well. T-scores have a mean (average) of 50 and a standard deviation of 10.

T-score classification systems usually will be different for different tests because the classification systems are determined by the test authors and publisher. Parents and teachers are not expected to know what the different T-score classifications used with various tests mean, and it really isn't necessary. The reason is that the scores will be interpreted and explained in the report.

Table 5 provides two examples of T-score classification systems that might be used for two different personality tests or behavioral checklists.

Table 5

Examples of How T-score Classification Systems
Might Look for Different Tests

Example 1:	**T-score**	**Classification**
	70+	Very Elevated
	65–69	Elevated
	60–64	High Average
	40–59	Average
	<40	Low
Example 2:	**T-score**	**Classification**
	70+	Significantly Elevated
	60–69	Elevated
	55–59	High Average
	<55	Average

Scaled Score

A *scaled score* is yet another common type of standard score. Scaled scores range from 1 to 19 and have a mean (average) of 10 and a standard deviation of 3. Like all standard scores, scaled scores tell you whether a score is above average, average, or below average. Where will you see scaled scores? The subtests used in IQ tests are usually where scaled scores are used. Subtests are the smaller tests that make up the IQ test. Table 6 shows how scaled scores are typically classified:

Table 6

A Scaled Score Classification System

Scaled Score	Classification
16–19	Superior
13–15	Above Average
8–12	Average
5–7	Below Average
1–4	Significantly Below Average

Standard scores, stanines, and T-scores are popular in educational and psychological reports, but one score—the percentile—is also used a lot in test reports and is a particular favorite among educators. That alone is reason enough to become familiar with this score.

Percentile (or Percentile Rank)

The percentile (also called *percentile rank*) ranges from 1 to 99 (actually 99.9); there is no percentile of 100. The most important thing to keep in mind about a percentile is that it is *not* the same as percent or percentage. *Percents or percentages are used with classroom tests; percentiles are used with standardized tests.* If a child receives a 75% on a classroom test, it simply means that he or she answered 75% of the test questions correctly. But if a child scored at the 75th *percentile* on a standardized test, it means that he or she scored *higher* on the test than 75% of the students of the same age or grade who took the same test when it was being developed (normed). If a student scored at the 62nd percentile, it means that he or she scored higher than 62% of the students. And so on. So, the percentile tells you what percent *higher* a child scored compared to other students of the same age or grade who took the test.

When looking over testing results, you might see terms such as "local percentile," or "state percentile," or "national percentile." This means that the child was compared to groups of students locally, statewide, or nation-wide. And the percentile tells you what percent *higher* a child scored than the students in these groups.

Even after reading about percentile ranks, it's sometimes easy to become confused. That's because we are conditioned to think in terms of percentages, not percentiles. For example, if a child receives a score that is at the 45th percentile, you might think this is below average, but it's average for a percentile. Look at Table 7. Notice that the 45th percentile rank corresponds to a stanine of 5, which is solidly within the Average range.

Table 7

Comparison of Percentiles and Stanines

Percentile Rank	Stanine	Classification
96 & above	9	Very High
89–95	8	Above Average
77–88	7	Above Average
60–76	6	Average
40–59	5	Average
23–39	4	Average
11–22	3	Below Average
4–10	2	Below Average
Below 4	1	Very Low

This chart will be useful when looking over a child's testing report because it will help to make sense out of what at first may seem like a hodgepodge of numbers. Because most proficiency tests use stanines and percentiles, you might want to keep this chart handy.

Grade Equivalent

A *grade equivalent (GE)* is the student's test score expressed in *grade levels*. The child's score on a test is compared to the average score obtained by students in the *different grades*. For instance, if a student in the ninth grade received a grade equivalent of 10.5 on a standardized test, this means that his or her performance on the test is similar to the *average* score of students half way through the tenth grade. Not bad—that's above average for a ninth grader. If the grade equivalent score was 6.0, it means that his or her performance on the test is similar to the *average* score of students beginning the sixth grade, which would be below average for a ninth-grade student.

Caution must be used when interpreting grade equivalents. Many people believe that a grade equivalent tells us the grade in which a student should be placed. It does not. If a fifth-grade student receives a grade equivalent of 8.0, it does not mean they should be placed in the eighth grade. It means he or she is above average when compared to children in the fifth grade.

Age Equivalent

Age equivalent (AE) is sometimes referred to as mental age, and it's another score sometimes seen in reports. It is similar to grade equivalent but refers to the student's test score expressed in *age levels* instead of grade levels. With age equivalents, the student's score on a test is compared to the average score obtained by students of *different ages*. So, if a 10-year-old receives an age equivalent score of 14.0 (which is 14 years–0 months), it means this score is similar to the *average* score of students who just turned 14 years of age. It's above average. Likewise, if a 16-year-old boy receives an age equivalent of 12.0 (12 years–0 months), it clearly shows that he is behind his age peers because his score is the same as the *average* score obtained by children who just turned 12 years of age.

It's best to stay away from interpreting an age equivalent as representing a student's true mental age. For example, it would not be accurate to assume that a 15-year-old student with an age equivalent of 11-0 (11 years–0 months) has the mental age of an 11-year-old. That's because at age 15, the student likely has had more (and different) life experiences than the average 11-year-old. And these life experiences are things not measured by tests.

35

Standard Age Score

The *Standard Age Score (SAS)* is a type of standard score used on certain tests such as the Cognitive Abilities Test (CogAT) published by the Riverside Publishing Company. The CogAT is a group test that measures a student's reasoning *abilities* in three areas: 1) verbal, 2) quantitative (math), and 3) nonverbal (analyzing geometric shapes and figures). Because it measures abilities rather than skills in specific school subjects, for all intents and purposes it could be considered an IQ test (and some teachers treat it as such), although it is not billed as one.

The CogAT has a mean (average) of 100 and a standard deviation of 16, and most IQ tests have a mean of 100 and a standard deviation of 15. (See explanation of standard deviation on pages 38–40.) These statistical similarities and the fact that the CogAT and IQ tests both measure *abilities* make it understandable why the CogAT is sometimes regarded as an IQ test.

What does the SAS tell you? In general, a simple way to interpret the SAS is like this: The more the SAS is above the average of 100, the faster the student's rate/speed of learning; the more the SAS is below 100, the slower the student's rate/speed of learning.

As a side note, the CogAT is often administered in conjunction with the Iowa Tests of Basic Skills (ITBS), also published by the Riverside Publishing Company. The ITBS is a popular group achievement test that measures skill levels in school subject areas such as reading and math.

Why are these two measures—reasoning abilities (CogAT) and achievement skills (ITBS)—often administered together? The reason is so that parents and educators can get an estimate of what their child or student is capable of doing (based on their ability scores) and whether he or she is learning up to that level (based on their achievement scores).

A significant difference between a child's ability level and achievement level may alert teachers to potential problems. For example, when ability is much higher than achievement, this could indicate a problem with motivation or perhaps even a learning problem. When ability level is much lower than achievement, this could mean that the student didn't try very hard on the ability test, but on a more positive note it also could indicate a highly motivated student.

Normal Curve Equivalent

The *Normal Curve Equivalent (NCE)* is a type of score that ranges from 1 to 99, just like percentiles. But NCEs have equal intervals between scores; percentiles do not. For example, the distance between NCEs of 10 and 20 is the *same* as the distance between NCEs of 30 and 40, or between 40 and 50, and so on. But the distance between percentiles of 10 and 20 is *not* the same as the distance between percentiles of 30 and 40, or between 40 and 50, and so on. This "equal interval" characteristic of NCEs means they can be averaged, which makes it easier to compare the results from different achievement tests and to evaluate overall school progress.

The NCE is used primarily for research purposes, so unless you're conducting research or evaluating government programs, there really is little need to know about the NCE. The reason it's included here is because you may see it from time to time, and when you do, you'll at least have an idea of what it is.

Zone of Proximal Development

Occasionally you may hear your child's teacher refer to something called the ZPD, which stands for the *Zone of Proximal Development*. Despite the technical-sounding name, the ZPD is simply an estimated "comfort zone" for reading. It's based on a student's grade-equivalent score on a reading test. For example, if a student received a grade-equivalent of 4.5 on the test, the ZPD for this score might be a grade-level reading range of 3.2 to 5.0. This means that reading material below 3.2 is likely to be too easy and not challenging enough, and anything above 5.0 is likely to be too difficult. The ZPD is typically used to help students select books they can comfortably read and understand.

What's a Standard Deviation?

Standard deviation is a common testing term. It's an important one, too, but mainly to psychologists and other test experts. The problem for parents is that the term "standard deviation" is so casually tossed about at meetings where test results are discussed that they think they should know what it means. But parents can understand their children's test scores without having the foggiest idea of what a standard deviation means.

Let's look at two examples of how a psychologist or other testing profes-sional might explain the testing results of an imaginary student, Peggy, to her imaginary parents, Mr. & Mrs. Frapp. The statements are exactly alike except for the underlined passage.

Example 1

Mr. and Mrs. Frapp, your daughter Peggy's IQ is 115. This falls one standard deviation above the mean. This score is above average and falls at the 84th percentile rank. This means that she scored higher than 84% of the students in her age group. She's a bright girl.

Example 2

Mr. and Mrs. Frapp, your daughter Peggy's IQ is 115. This score is above average and falls at the 84th percentile rank. This means that she scored higher than 84% of the students in her age group. She's a bright girl.

Example 2 provides enough useful information without confusing the reader. If you're the curious sort and want to know what a standard deviation is, here's a fairly simple explanation.

The standard deviation is a measure of the dispersion of a set of scores from the average (also called the *mean* in statistical terms); it tells us how far the scores are spread out. For example, if a group of students who took an IQ test all got the same score, then the standard devia-tion would be zero because there is no dispersion. This would be a rarity. It's more likely that the scores would be different, or spread out. The less spread out the scores, the smaller the standard deviation (and the more reliable the test); the more spread out the scores, the larger the standard deviation (and the less reliable the test).

Table 8 also explains the standard deviation in terms of its relationship to standard scores and percentile ranks. It shows how many standard deviations a score is from the mean (average) as well as the corresponding percentile rank. Again, this information is not essential to understanding test results; it's being presented merely for the benefit of those who might be interested in a more detailed explanation.

Table 8

Relationship between Standard Deviation,
Standard Score, and Percentile Rank

Standard Deviations from the Mean	IQ or Achievement Test Standard Scores	Percentile Rank
+3	145	99.87
+2	130	98
+1	115	84
0	100 (Mean)	50
-1	85	16
-2	70	2
-3	55	.13

The above information applies to test scores that are "normally distributed" or "bell-shaped," which covers most scores on standardized tests. Figure 1 shows what this chart looks like when drawn as a normal or bell-shaped curve.

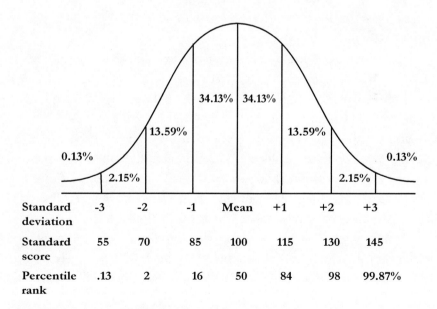

Figure 1. Relationship between normal curve, standard deviation, standard score, and percentile rank.

Notice that approximately 34% of the population have IQs or achievement test scores (standard scores) between 100 and 115, and approximately 34% have scores between 85 and 100. Likewise, approximately 14% have scores between 70 and 85, and 14% also have scores between 115 and 130. And approximately 2% of the population have IQs that are either very high (above 130) or very low (below 70).

If you look at the percentile ranks, you'll notice that an IQ of 130 falls at the 98th percentile rank (or higher than 98% of the population), an IQ of 115 is at the 84th percentile rank (or higher than 84% of the population), an IQ of 100 is at the 50th percentile rank (or higher than 50% of the population), and so on. The importance of this normal curve information is that it gives you an idea where a student stands in relation to others in the population.

As we discussed earlier, a characteristic of the normal curve is that it's shaped like a bell (see Figure 1), which is why it's sometimes called the *bell curve*. With a normal curve, most scores fall toward the middle, which means that most people's test scores will cluster around the mean or average. As we move toward the ends of the curve, we find that only a small percentage of people have test scores that are very high (130 or higher) or very low (70 or lower).

As a parent, your goal is to understand your child's testing results, not to become a statistical expert, so don't fret if you don't completely understand the normal curve. The important thing is to have the courage to ask questions if you don't understand where your child stands in terms of their test scores. Is their score above average? Average? Below average? How far above or below average? What do these results mean for your child? Do the results point to any problems? Does your child need any special interventions, or tutoring? Do the results accurately represent your child's skills and abilities? For many parents the question is as simple as whether their child is learning.

Many parents are afraid of asking what they fear may be a silly question, or they just don't want to bother school personnel, who genuinely seem to be so busy. Some parents are intimidated by the formality of school meetings. But you may be surprised to find that teachers, school counselors, principals, and psychologists are usually very willing to answer parents' questions. If you do come across someone who is less than cooperative or simply cannot answer your questions, don't give up. Ask to speak with someone who can help.

The better you understand testing results, the better you'll be able to make informed decisions about your child's education. You'll be able to determine if the results are being used appropriately or interpreted correctly, or whether the results are even relevant to certain educational decisions. You'll also be in a better position to challenge educational decisions if necessary. Your role will be that of an active, informed parent rather than that of a parent who places blind faith in the "system" and obediently follows its advice. In the end, you will become an important part of the checks and balances.

CHAPTER 3

Intelligence Tests

It's the day of the high-school reunion. The woman who just a few weeks ago was excited about meeting her former classmates and friends, many of whom she had not seen in 30 years, suddenly found herself questioning whether she should go at all. She was successful in her career and by all appearances seemed to be doing well in life. Encouraged by her family, she reluctantly agreed to attend. Shortly after arriving at the reunion, the woman was surprised when one of her former classmates greeted her with, "Hey, I remember you. You were always very smart." With that statement, her anxieties dissolved and she ended up having a great time. It's very flattering when someone refers to us as smart. It makes us feel good about ourselves.

Society places a premium on being smart. We see smart people as high achievers and successful in life. (And, indeed, as a group, smart people do relatively well in life.) Next to physical attractiveness, perhaps no other human characteristic is as cherished as high intelligence. But what is intelligence, and how important is it?

What Is Intelligence?

Attempts to define intelligence date back over a hundred years. You would think that by now we'd have a definition of intelligence on which experts agree. Surprisingly, though, we don't. In fact, psychologists have never been able to agree on how to define it. There is good reason for this—intelligence is a complex concept.

One common definition of intelligence, which we will use for our discussion, is this: The ability to reason, solve problems, and understand the world in which we live. Intelligence tests, or what most people refer to as IQ (Intelligence Quotient) tests, contain specific tasks and questions that attempt to measure these abilities.

Most people consider intelligence and IQ to be the same, but techni-cally they're not. As mentioned above, intelligence is a complex concept that covers a wide range of abilities, whereas IQ is merely a score on an IQ test that supposedly represents those abilities. In other words, an IQ is a measure, or index, of how smart or intelligent a person is.

How Important Is IQ?

Just about everyone agrees that IQ is important. But just how important is it? IQ is strongly related to the three elements included in the above definition of intelligence—the ability to reason, to solve problems, and to understand the world in which we live. The higher an individual's IQ, the better they will be able to do these things. This typically will lead to more accomplish-ments and successes in life. Generally speaking, persons with higher IQs will learn at a faster rate. They also will grasp abstract concepts and complex material more easily.

But IQ's ability to predict is limited. It cannot predict specific life successes, such as who will write great novels, who will become an Olympic athlete, or who will achieve a level of fame like that of certain actors, musicians, or professional athletes. Nor can it predict who will attain eminence or great-ness like that known only by the world's greatest scientists and philosophers.

In all fairness to IQ tests, they never were intended to be used to predict these types of specific successes. In fact, no such test exists. Although IQ does a reasonably good job of predicting success in general, it's difficult to determine in any specific way how a person will ultimately turn out. That's because a person is a complex combination of unique experiences, emo-tions, thoughts, beliefs, attitudes, motivation, interests, stamina, desires, and more. These things impact an individual in important ways. They are the nonintellectual aspects of our lives, and they should always be taken into consideration when looking at what leads to success. A person may have an average IQ, but that same person may be a gifted dancer or singer and be able to perform their art superbly, which is something that cannot be measured by standardized tests.

These nonintellectual influences serve as important reminders that we live in a vibrant and complex world, not in a vacuum. They tell us that humans are multifaceted and dynamic creatures whose lives are influenced by an intricate and sometimes delicate interplay of many factors rather than a single factor such as IQ.

How IQ Tests Are Administered

Have you ever wondered how IQ tests are administered? Some people think that they're just like school tests where a student reads questions from a booklet and marks their answers on a bubble answer sheet with a #2 pencil. That's basically true for group-administered IQ tests, but individually administered IQ tests are a different breed. With these tests, as the name suggests, the examiner meets individually with the child, who is asked to perform a variety of tasks (e.g., working with blocks, putting pictures in order, answering vocabulary questions) rather than marking answers on a piece of paper.

Whether a child is given an individual or a group IQ test may not seem like an important matter, but it is. Let's take a closer look at these two ways of administering IQ tests and find out why.

Individually Administered IQ Tests

Individually administered IQ tests are specifically designed to be administered to one person at a time. They are among the most reliable and most accurate of all psychological tests. They are the first choice for situations where important decisions are to be made, such as when making or confirming a diagnosis or deciding on an educational placement.

Individually administered IQ testing usually is conducted in an office or room where distractions are minimal. Establishing rapport with the child by discussing his or her interests is an important first step when testing a child because this creates a positive relationship between the examiner and child, which is likely to motivate the child to put forth their best effort. And because individually administered IQ tests provide an excellent opportunity to closely observe a child's behaviors, the examiner is able to determine whether the results are valid and accurately represent his or her level of intelligence.

Individually administered IQ tests often include a verbal portion and a nonverbal portion. On the verbal portion, the examiner may ask the child questions related to vocabulary, analogies, verbal reasoning, or other verbal area. The nonverbal portion usually involves having the child work with blocks, puzzles, picture cards, geometric designs, or other hands-on task. Because some of the nonverbal tasks are timed, a stopwatch is used to accurately record the time it takes to complete a task. Some tests go beyond the basic verbal and nonverbal distinction and include tasks related to memory and attention, and processing speed (how quickly and efficiently a child can perform mental operations).

An individual IQ test can take anywhere from 1 to 2 hours to complete. That can be a long time for younger children who tire easily or those who find it difficult to concentrate. In these cases, the test may need to be given over two separate testing sessions.

Occasionally an individual IQ test is the only test that needs to be administered, as might be the case when evaluating a child for a gifted program. It's more common, though, for these tests to be included as part of a comprehensive evaluation. This comprehensive evaluation usually includes detailed interviews, a developmental history, classroom observations, and administering several other types of tests such as personality tests and achievement tests, all in addition to the IQ test. Because a comprehensive evaluation can take several hours to complete, they usually are conducted over a period of days. This is to avoid the child from becoming overly tired, which could lead to inaccurate test results.

Group Administered IQ Tests

Schools are the main users of group IQ tests, and using these tests offers clear benefits. The main advantage is that a large number of children can be evaluated in a short period of time, usually 30 to 60 minutes. An added bonus is the small investment of professional resources. For example, a single teacher can administer a group test to hundreds of students.

Besides these administrative benefits, group IQ tests also can provide useful information to educators. They can:

- provide teachers and principals a rough estimate of students' abilities; this gives some idea of what can be expected in terms of classroom achievement, and

- determine if a child should be referred for a more comprehensive evaluation, such as for giftedness or intellectual disability.

Group IQ tests sometimes are included as part of school-wide standardized achievement testing programs. Although they're not called IQ tests when used in this manner, for all intents and purposes that's what they are. But don't go searching for the term "IQ" anywhere on the computerized report sent home from school. You won't find it. Instead, you're likely to see a term such as "cognitive ability" or something similar. In educational settings, the terms "cognitive ability" and "IQ" mean the same. The reason "cognitive ability" is preferred over "IQ" is because IQ implies inherited ability and conveys the idea that children cannot learn more than what is indicated by their IQ. Of course, children can learn more, and in many instances a lot more.

The reliability and validity of group administered IQ tests generally are not as good as their individually administered counterparts. Therefore, group IQ tests should be thought of as providing only a very general estimate of a child's level of intelligence. That's why these tests should not be used to make important decisions. In instances where important decisions are to be made, individually administered IQ tests should be the preferred choice and even then usually as part of a comprehensive evaluation.

Another issue related to group IQ tests, or any group test for that matter, is that rapport cannot be effectively established as it can with individually administered tests. There also is little opportunity to keep a close eye on each child while they're taking the test. Because of this, it's difficult to know whether a child is really trying his or her best or whether nervousness, inattention, or other issue is affecting their performance.

Classifications Based On IQ Scores

Classification systems are important in the area of educational and psychological testing because they give meaning to the scores. For example, if you received a report from the school psychologist stating only that your son's recent testing showed that he had an IQ of 102, what would that tell you? Very little. Now, if the report said that he received an IQ of 102 and that this score falls in the Average range, then that would give you more meaningful information.

Table 9 shows a typical standard score classification system used with many popular intelligence/IQ tests. (You may recognize this as the same system presented in Chapter 2.) As you will see in the next chapter, this classification system also is used with many standardized achievement tests. Most intelligence and achievement tests use the same basic standard score classification system in order to make comparisons between a student's level of intellectual functioning and their achievement skills easier to interpret. Often the only difference between an IQ test and an achievement test classification system will be slightly different names for the classification categories; the standard score ranges usually are the same.

Table 9

Typical Classification System for IQ Tests

Standard Score	Classification
130 and higher	Very Superior
120-129	Superior
110-119	High Average
90-109	Average
80-89	Low Average
70-79	Borderline
69 and lower	Significantly Below Average

The IQ categories and the approximate percentage of persons in the population falling within each category or IQ range are shown in Figure 2. Again, notice that the largest percentage of people fall within the Average range (yes, most people have an average IQ), and the smallest percentages fall at the highest and lowest ends—the Very Superior and Significantly Below Average ranges (few people have very low or very high IQs).

Another interesting point relates to the shape of the graph. If you were to connect the top of each category in the graph with a continuous line, you would see that the shape of the graph resembles a bell. You may recall from our earlier discussions that this shape is referred to as the "bell curve" or "bell-shaped curve." Another common name is the "normal curve."

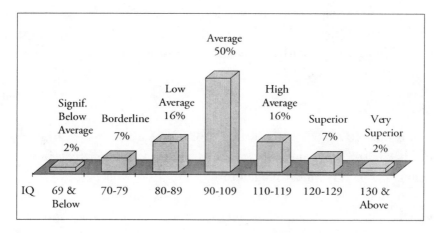

Figure 2. Approximate percentage of the population within each IQ range.

What the IQ Ranges Tell Us

What follows is general information on the IQ ranges. This information assumes the child has no disability that would interfere with learning. As you read about these categories, keep in mind that scores that are close together are not really different from one another in any practical way, even though they may fall in different classifications. For instance, although an IQ of 108 is within the Average range (90-109) and an IQ of 111 is within the High Average range (110-119), no important difference exists between these two scores.

It's also a good idea to keep in mind that IQs are good but not perfect predictors. You may smile broadly after learning that your daughter's IQ was high enough to make her eligible for a gifted class, but you may be disappointed if she achieves less than you expected. Or you may be puzzled over why your neighbor's son with an average IQ is doing better in school than your son with an above average IQ. Or you may proudly think to yourself that your daughter's IQ of 120 means she is smarter than your neighbor's son who has an IQ of 118, when in reality no practical difference exists between these scores. And teachers may be confused when two students with the same IQ show very different levels of success in the classroom.

These inconsistencies usually can be explained by *individual differences*, which are characteristics unique to a child. They're a child's specific pattern of skills and intellectual abilities that interact with personality characteristics

49

such as motivation, determination, attitudes, beliefs, curiosity, fears and anxieties, and so on. Individual differences are what make a child "one of a kind." They are important, and they do affect scores. Now, let's take a closer look at the IQ ranges.

The Very Superior IQ (130+)

Approximately 2% of the population have IQs of 130 or higher. In general, children in this group do exceptionally well in school and often are involved with gifted or enrichment programs.

Although IQ tests are one of the main instruments used to identify gifted children, they identify only those who are intellectually gifted. What about those who are talented in music or art or mechanics, or the child who excels in science? Because IQ tests do not measure these areas, other tests or methods of identification need to be used, such as aptitude tests, achievement tests, portfolios, auditions, teacher observations and recommendations, and the student's notable past and present accomplishments. For example, a child suspected of being gifted in writing could be given an IQ test, but the results would not be particularly meaningful. A better approach would be to have the student submit writing samples which are judged by a panel of writing experts.

Using standardized tests also could present problems in identifying giftedness in children with learning problems. A child with a learning disability, for example, may never score high enough on an IQ or achievement test to be eligible for a gifted program but nonetheless may be quite gifted. This is another reason why it is important not to rely solely on tests when making important decisions.

The Superior IQ (120–129)

Children whose IQ scores fall between 120 to 129 could be considered "almost gifted" intellectually. In fact, some children in this group may be gifted by other measures but their IQ simply may not reach the cutoff set by the school system.

Individuals whose IQs fall within this range also make up a relatively small percentage of the population—approximately 7%. These children clearly are very bright and typically excel in the classroom but may not qualify for gifted or enrichment programs that rely only on IQ scores to determine eligibility. This can be frustrating for these children because, like their gifted classmates, they may become bored in the classroom unless they are presented with challenging activities. Parents, too, become frustrated because the responsibility of nurturing their "almost gifted" falls almost entirely on them, with little or no guidance from school.

The High Average IQ (110–119)

Children with IQs between 110 and 119 also are "bright." The IQs of approximately 16% of the population fall within this range. IQs in this range may not seem especially high because we're so accustomed to hearing only about individuals with the highest IQs, that is, those with IQs of 130 or higher. But to get an idea of just how intellectually capable children in the high average range are, consider this: An IQ of 115 is higher than the IQs of approximately 84% of the population. That's a respectable level of performance by just about any measure.

Like the child with a superior IQ (120-129), the child with a high average IQ generally will not be involved with any type of enrichment program at school but will have to rely on guidance and encouragement from family and on self-motivation to avoid boredom. Children with IQs in the high average range typically do very well in the classroom.

The Average IQ (90–109)

If you were to look up "average" in a dictionary, you would find definitions such as "typical," "common," or "ordinary." Although these are not necessarily negative terms, they also are not words that usually convey a sense of quality. For example, if we have a health problem, we want to be treated by a good doctor, not an average one. We want our children to attend good schools, not average ones. When we go to a nice restaurant, we expect good food, not an average meal. And when college graduates begin their job search, they hope to land a good job, not an average one. Clearly, the word "average" is not considered a term of endearment.

Society's view of average in our day-to-day lives understandably has flowed over into the IQ/intelligence arena, but it doesn't always apply. It would be inaccurate, for example, to say that children of average intelligence are destined to get only average grades in school or only average scores on standardized proficiency or achievement tests. It would be equally inaccurate to say that they cannot be very successful in life.

People with average IQs can be found in many different careers (from unskilled workers to professionals) and at many different levels of success (from business failures to millionaires). Like individuals in other IQ groups, persons with average IQs who are hard-working, determined, and persistent in pursuing their goals and who understand their unique strengths and weaknesses generally will be more successful and will accomplish more in life than they would otherwise.

Average as it applies to IQ or intelligence covers a lot of territory. Figure 2 shows that approximately 50% of the population will have IQs within the average range—IQs between 90 and 109. The "average" child's classroom performance can range from below average to above average, depending on his or her personality characteristics (e.g., level of ambition, persistence, motivation) and unique skills and abilities.

One of the surest ways for a child of average intelligence to get good grades is by being diligent with studying, assuming the child has no disability that interferes with learning. And one of the surest ways of getting above average scores on standardized proficiency/achievement tests is to develop effective study habits early in life. Everyone has to study in order to learn. No one is born with knowledge. It is true, however, that some children will have to study longer in order to achieve at a level similar to that of their faster-learning peers.

The Low Average IQ (80–89)

Individuals whose levels of intelligence fall within the 80 and 89 IQ range make up approximately 16% of the population. Educators sometimes refer to these children as "slow learners." These children will learn, but the speed at which they learn and their ability to grasp complex or abstract concepts typically lags behind higher IQ children. Children in this group can easily become discouraged and develop a dislike for school. That's understandable. They spend a great deal of time and effort trying to keep up with their classmates and become frustrated when their efforts are rewarded with poor grades.

Our educational system is geared toward teaching the average student. (The exceptions are students receiving special education services or those in gifted or enrichment programs.) Consequently, children with abilities in the 80-89 IQ range easily can feel frustrated, forgotten, and left behind.

The Borderline IQ (70–79)

The number of individuals in the general population whose IQs fall between 70 and 79 is about 7%. The learning difficulties of children in this group usually are readily apparent. Their rate of learning is much slower and their level of classroom achievement typically is significantly behind their same-age classmates. Many of these students will struggle in the regular classroom just to receive a barely passing mark. A fair percentage of these students will require some level of special education instruction in order to learn at a rate consistent with their abilities rather than having them fall further and further behind in their studies.

Children with IQs in this range often are incorrectly referred to as "borderline mentally retarded." The correct term is "borderline intellectual functioning." Some of these children, though, eventually may be diagnosed with intellectual disability (formerly referred to as mental retardation), but that will come from the results of a comprehensive evaluation rather than the results of a single test.

Classification of Persons with Intellectual Disability

The term "mental retardation" has been used for decades, but it's now considered to be outdated. According to the American Association on Intellectual and Developmental Disabilities (AAIDD), formerly known as the American Association on Mental Retardation (AAMR), the currently preferred term for mental retardation is *intellectual disability*. This term more accurately describes the disability, and it also carries fewer negative associations.

Because the AAIDD is the foremost authority on intellectual disability, it makes sense to look to them for a definition. According to AAIDD, an intellectual disability exists when a person has significant limitations in intellectual functioning and in adaptive behavior functioning occurring before the age of 18 (Schalock et al., 2010).

"Limitations in intellectual functioning" means having an IQ of 70 or lower (but the IQ can be as high as 75), as measured by an individually administered IQ test; approximately 2% of the general population have IQs of 70 or lower. But having an IQ of 70 to 75 or lower by itself is insufficient to make a diagnosis of intellectual disability. As the above definition points out, limitations in adaptive behavior functioning also must be present.

"Limitations in adaptive behavior functioning" means having significantly below average self-help or independent living skills. These are the skills needed to take care of oneself in order to live independently. According to the AAIDD definition, adaptive behaviors include "conceptual, social, and practical skills." Examples of *conceptual skills* include expressing oneself, understanding others, reading and writing, making decisions for oneself, and dealing with money; *social skills* examples include interacting with people, understanding potential hazards and threats, following rules, and obeying laws; and examples of *practical skills* include toileting, dressing and feeding oneself, using transportation, housekeeping skills, and work skills. (Tests of adaptive behavior will be discussed briefly in Chapter 7.)

The AAIDD view of intellectual disability goes even beyond an individual's levels of intellectual and adaptive behavior functioning. It also takes into consideration the specific strengths and limitations of the individual in the context of their environment as well as the degree to which they require supports that will foster and maintain personal growth. Supports can be provided by parents, by professionals such as psychologists, social workers, and counselors, or by community agencies.

Another system of classification of intellectual disabilities is that developed by the American Psychiatric Association (2000) and published in the *Diagnostic and Statistical Manual of Mental Disorders–Fourth Edition–Text Revision (DSM-IV-TR)*. The *DSM-IV-TR* uses the older term "mental retardation," but it is expected that "intellectual disability" will be used in the DSM-V due out in 2013. The *DSM-IV-TR* system is the diagnostic standard for all mental health professionals in the United States and is widely used in psychiatric settings, clinics, hospitals, and private practices.

The *DSM-IV-TR* classification system is similar to the AAIDD system to the extent that it also requires substantial deficits in intellectual functioning (an IQ of approximately 70 or lower) and in adaptive behavior functioning (self-help/independent living skills), which must occur before age 18 years. The individual's scores on these measures determines four levels of severity of mental retardation: mild, moderate, severe, and profound. A fifth classification category—*Mental Retardation, Severity Unspecified*—is used when an intellectual disability is strongly suspected but the individual is unable to be tested by standard methods.

Although "intellectual disability" is less perjorative than "mental retardation," it's still a diagnosis and is not likely to be used in school reports unless originating from a mental health professional in the community. Instead, you're likely to see more traditional educational terms, such as "cognitively impaired," "cognitively delayed," "developmental disability," or "developmentally delayed."

Issues in Intelligence Testing

Among the most contentious issues in all of testing are those related to intelligence. The question of whether intelligence is determined by heredity or the environment usually receives top billing. Other issues also are worth discussing, not only because of their controversial nature but because they are downright interesting. These include whether IQ measures potential, whether more than one type of intelligence exists, whether intelligence increases naturally from generation to generation, and whether IQ can be enhanced. Let's begin with the classic nature–nurture controversy.

Nature versus Nurture

The nature (heredity) versus nurture (environment) debate is rooted in the 1859 publication of Charles Darwin's *Origin of Species*. Many of the more recent controversies, though, can be traced to a 1969 article by educational psychologist Arthur Jensen, entitled, "How Much Can We Boost IQ and Scholastic Achievement?" published in the *Harvard Educational Review*. The major thrust of the article was that general ability (intelligence) has a high degree of heritability—as much as 80%. (Heritability is the degree to which an attribute—in this case intelligence—is inherited.)

As expected, Jensen's article created considerable furor at the time. College professors, civil rights activists, political activists, and even the person on the street were heatedly debating what came to be known as the "nature–nurture controversy," occasionally with charges of racism thrown about.

Why all the uproar over whether intelligence is due to heredity or environment? And what relevance does it have for parents and teachers? The reason for the uproar is that a hereditarian explanation for intelligence is like saying that one's life is written in stone and can't be changed in any substantive way, even with effort. A hereditarian view justifies (though wrongly) claims of superiority of one person over another, one group of people over another, one nation over another.

To believe that intelligence is based solely on one's genetic endowment steals the hopes and dreams of millions of children. It can lower expectations at home and in the classroom and keep a child from reaching higher goals. This simple belief can even reach into neighborhood playgrounds where it subconsciously drives hurtful attacks of "stupid" and "dumb."

Although the nature-nurture debate has been going on for more than a century, neither side has ever been declared the unequivocal winner. Most professionals have come to accept the more balanced and scientifically sound explanation that intelligence is influenced by an interplay of hereditary and environmental factors. That balance, though, teetered a bit with the 1994 publication of *The Bell Curve: Intelligence and Class Structure in American Life* by Richard J. Herrnstein and Charles Murray. Herrnstein and Murray again raised the idea that IQ/intelligence is largely inherited and that success (or lack of success) in many areas of life is directly related to an individual's level of intelligence. Moreover, they asserted that the difference in IQ scores between blacks and whites is largely due to heredity.

The Bell Curve is almost 900 pages long and loaded with statistics, charts, and an impressive list of references. It easily could come across as the definitive work on the heritability of intelligence, settling once and for all this age-old controversy.

But *The Bell Curve* has not gone unchallenged. In fact, entire books have been written disputing *The Bell Curve's* ideas. One such book is the *The Bell Curve Wars: Race, Intelligence, and the Future of America* (1994), which devoted all 19 of its chapters from authors of various backgrounds to dispute Herrnstein and Murray's notion on the heritability of intelligence. One chapter author, psychologist Richard Nisbett, describes Herrnstein and Murray's evidence as "missing, misdescribed, and oddly-interpreted" (p. 54). Another chapter contributor, psychologist Howard Gardner, sees the same apparent flaw, noting that Herrnstein and Murray's view that heredity largely dictates our lives is based on old-world ideas and should be taken with a grain of salt.

It's easy to be lured into taking sides on the nature-nurture debate, but neither position alone adequately explains the make-up of intelligence. What role does each play? In his 2005 book, *The Ethical Brain*, noted neuroscientist and psychologist Michael S. Gazzaniga cites research on twins that rather convincingly supports the view that the contribution of heredity and environment to intelligence is approximately 50 percent each. Many scientists agree that this is a reasonable estimate. An important point to keep in mind, though, is that the contributions of heredity and environment do not operate in isolation or independent of one another. Rather, intelligence is affected by an interplay of environment and heredity.

Fixed versus Growth Views of Intelligence

New and exciting ideas are being discussed in the halls of academia, and the good news is that these ideas are filtering down into our everyday lives. In her 2002 book, *Why Smart People Can Be So Stupid*, psychologist Carol S. Dweck describes how the various theories of intelligence actually could be classified in two basic ways. One way assumes that intelligence is a fixed trait that remains basically the same from an early age through adulthood. The other is that intelligence can be enhanced with effort. In her 2006 book, *Mindset: The New Psychology of Success*, Dweck aptly describes these two views as the *fixed* and *growth* mindsets.

The distinction between these two views has important practical implications for children (and adults). Dweck (2006) notes that children who adopt the fixed mindset tend to tie failure to their self-worth and, therefore, avoid challenges where failure is a possibility. Consequently, they often avoid new challenges and instead stick with safe tasks where success is assured. Fixed mindset children are highly invested in protecting their egos and avoid situations in which they might be perceived as unintelligent. This limits the number of learning opportunities available to them and stifles intellectual growth.

Children who believe in the growth view of intelligence also feel disappointment over failures, but their particular perspective gives them distinct advantages. For one, they do not allow failures to threaten their self-worth. Instead, they look for ways that could help them meet future challenges. They also approach challenging activities with more confidence and are not frightened by the prospect of making mistakes. (Mistakes, after all, are a natural part of learning.) As a result, they generally have more learning opportunities. This translates into generally better academic performance and more successes than children with a fixed view of intelligence.

Mindset is also related to motivation. A growth mindset person, for example, is likely to be more motivated than someone with a fixed mindset, and therefore will likely have more accomplishments and successes in life. Motivation is important in just about everything we do and may be the single most important characteristic related to success. Even with something as complex as creativity, it's motivation, and not simply innate ability or talent, that researchers now consider to be the key element to producing creative works. In his 2006 book, *Explaining Creativity: The Science of Human Innovation*, psychologist and creativity researcher R. Keith Sawyer writes, "The most important predictor of creative output is hard work, dedication, and intrinsic motivation" (p. 54).

Does IQ Measure A Person's Potential?

A common misconception about an IQ test is that it measures potential. It does not. Potential is the most that a person is capable of learning. It's their maximum level of performance—the best he or she can ever expect to do. No test can measure that. To make such a claim is saying that we know exactly where the outer limits of human abilities are, and we don't.

Let's look at this more closely using the concept of overachievement. Overachievement is when a child learns more than predicted by their IQ. An example of overachievement would be when a student with an average IQ gets As or Bs in school, or receives above average test scores. If IQ truly measured potential, these types of performance patterns would never happen because a person could not learn more than they are capable of learning. But consider the real-life case of a high school junior with an average IQ who got a nearly perfect score on the math section of the SAT, or a 12-year-old boy with a below average IQ who scored significantly above average on the math portion of a standardized achievement test. These are not isolated instances; similar cases can be found in every school in the country.

The expectation that a person cannot achieve higher than what is predicted by their IQ places limits on people, and it stifles learning. Parents, teachers, or anyone entrusted with the responsibility of educating children should avoid this attitude. Having such expectations shows a failure to recognize the complex nature of human beings and the genuine influence that nonintellectual factors—such as motivation, curiosity, and determination—can have on success.

As noted in the previous section, this very point is emphasized by Dweck (2006), who notes that people tend to apply a fixed mindset view when it comes to thinking about test scores. The fixed mindset person, for example, treats IQ as an unchanging number and assumes that "one test can measure you forever." Dweck points to a serious problem with this view—it isn't true. She cites several famous people who had distinguished careers as adults but who were not particularly outstanding students as children.

Along similar lines, in the March 12, 2001 issue of *Time*, the SAT scores of several celebrities were listed, with the scores ranging from low to high. In looking over this list, one thing stands out—regardless of their score, each person was extraordinarily successful in their career.

The point here is that test scores do not come close to telling the whole story about a person's capabilities. But we don't have to look to celebrities to understand that we should not judge or define a person on the basis of their test scores. All we have to do is look in any classroom in America, where it's easy to find children achieving at levels higher, sometimes much higher, than their IQs would predict. The lesson is clear: In order to fully appreciate a child's capabilities, we must look beyond test scores.

Can IQ Be Boosted?

Another important issue in the area of intelligence, and an especially interesting one, is whether IQ can be increased. Imagine how life might be if we could boost intelligence. Students would do better on tests, their grades almost certainly would be better, and even their chances of success in life might improve. But is it possible to boost intelligence?

The work of Dweck mentioned earlier clearly suggests that adopting a growth mindset can enhance intelligence. Other factors can impact intelligence as well. Because much of the research has focused on the relationship between schooling and intelligence, that seems to be a good place to start.

Schooling and Intelligence

Common sense tells us that there should be a relationship between schooling and intelligence. But does the research bear this out? Stephen J. Ceci and Wendy M. Williams, in the October 1997 issue of *American Psychologist*, reported on their review of numerous studies and found these influences:

School attendance is important.
Students who attend school on a consistent basis generally show greater gains in IQ than those who attend school infrequently.

Starting school early has benefits.
Starting school early means the child will end up with more years of schooling, which tends to have a positive impact on IQ.

Dropping out of school has a negative effect.
Obviously, if a child quits school, the opportunity for learning decreases dramatically, and the opportunity for success in life decreases just as dramatically.

Summers off can have a negative effect.
Have you ever wondered why anyone would propose a 12-month school year? The reason is that IQ and achievement test scores show a slight decline over the summer months compared to end-of-school-year scores. The decline in scores tends to be greater for children whose summers lack educational activities, such as taking music lessons, reading interesting books, or visiting the zoo, museum, or library.

These findings are impressive, but they should not be taken to mean that IQ will increase substantially—let's say, 10 to 20 points—simply by starting school early, attending school regularly, not dropping out, attending summer school, or engaging in summer enrichment programs such as music lessons. These activities do seem to increase IQ scores, but the degree to which they do remains a point of contention among experts.

"Learning to Think" Programs

In the same issue of the *American Psychologist*, David N. Perkins and Tina A. Grotzer reviewed several studies on "learning to think" programs. These programs teach things such as decision-making skills, problem-solving skills, how to think critically, how to reason, how to use inventive and creative thinking, and how to organize one's thinking. Indeed, based on their review, it does appear that individuals can be taught to think better and raise their levels of intelligence. But this by no means is a definitive conclusion. Questions remain as to whether what is being taught is "genuine" intelligence, that is, whether the gains from these "learning to think" programs can be maintained once the program stops.

Top-Quality Education and Child Care from Infancy

It's well-known that poor children generally do not do as well on standardized IQ and achievement tests as children from middle or upper class families. In fact, some experts consider socioeconomic status (SES), defined as family income, to be the most important factor related to test performance—more important than the amount of money a school district spends on each student, more important than the quality of teaching, and more important than class size.

But what if children from disadvantaged homes were provided with excellent educational opportunities as well as high-quality childcare from the moment they were born? Would this make a difference? The answer is yes.

Campbell and Burchinal (2008) describe an early childhood educational program, called the Abecedarian Project, which provided intensive intervention to poor children from birth through age 5. The intensive intervention consisted of high-quality childcare and preschool five days a week on a year-round basis. Here's what the researchers found when the children reached age 21, compared to children who did not receive the intervention:

- Increases in reading and math achievement scores
- A modest increase in IQ
- Had more years of education
- Higher percentage attended college
- Lower percentage became teen parents

This study presents fairly convincing evidence that high-quality childcare and preschool can make an important difference in the lives of disadvantaged children. That in itself is not particularly surprising because previous research has shown similar results. But what's different about this research is that it shows that the benefits can be long-lasting. It also shows the potentially powerful influence of something that's within our ability to control—the environment.

Using "Smart Drugs"

What if you could simply take a pill to improve your memory? No longer would you forget where you placed your car keys, the names of people you meet, or the birthdates of family members and friends. Would you take such a pill?

Imagine that your son is scheduled to take a college admissions test next month. He's a good student and has applied to several highly selective colleges, but you're concerned if he will be able to perform at his best because he's always had a bit of a problem with attention and concentration. What if a "smart pill" were available that could enhance your son's attention and concentration and possibly increase his chances of getting higher test scores. Would you allow this?

These examples may sound like futuristic thinking, but they're closer to reality than many might realize. For example, in his 2005 book, *The Ethical Brain*, Michael S. Gazzaniga notes that several "cognitive enhancers" or "smart drugs" have already been submitted for FDA approval.

What is the promise of these "smart drugs?" Generally, it's to improve memory. And because memory has such an important role in intelligence, any improvement in memory is likely to result in a corresponding increase in intelligence.

Some memory-enhancing drugs are available now, but they are prescription drugs whose use is limited to persons with known diseases or health problems, not for healthy individuals. For example, drugs to treat patients with Alzheimer's disease and to improve the attention and concentration of persons diagnosed with Attention-Deficit/Hyperactivity Disorder (ADHD) have been available for some time.

The real question is how these "smart drugs" ultimately will be used. According to media reports, it's not uncommon for college-age students to use stimulant medications to increase attention, concentration, and memory when facing exams (Stix, 2009). And anecdotal reports of high-school students taking stimulant medications to help boost scores on college admission tests are plentiful.

But is the use of these "smart pills" a legitimate way to improve performance, or is it cheating? If we consider the drugs to be a form of mental steroid, then it might be considered cheating. If we think of using them as another form of personal enhancement, much like plastic surgery, then the cheating issue becomes moot.

Also, will these drugs be so expensive that they essentially will be available only to the wealthy? And what is the potential for abuse? Perhaps most important is what might be the risks and long-term effects of using these "smart pills," especially for children, who physically and cognitively are still developing. These are just some of the issues that must be addressed before more serious use of these drugs is considered.

Training in Working Memory

One may not have to resort to drugs to improve intelligence. An especially interesting study (Jaeggi, Buschkuehl, Jonides, & Perrig, 2008) published in *The Proceedings of the National Academy of Sciences* found that a certain kind of intelligence—fluid intelligence—can be increased with training. Specifically, this study demonstrated that when a sample of young adults was trained on a demanding working memory task, their fluid intelligence increased. (In its simplest form, working memory can be thought of as short-term or recent memory.) In fact, the more training the participants received, the more their fluid intelligence increased. What is so remarkable about this is that fluid intelligence is generally considered to be unaffected by learning or training. But before proceeding, a little background is in order.

Experts generally divide intelligence into two broad categories: 1) fluid intelligence, and 2) crystallized intelligence. Think of fluid intelligence as the ability you're born with; it's innate. Examples of fluid intelligence would be abstract reasoning and problem solving. Schooling or other life experiences supposedly have little effect on fluid intelligence. In contrast, crystallized intelligence is what we acquire through schooling and life experiences. As you might expect, studying and hard work can increase crystallized intelligence.

But if both fluid and crystallized intelligence can be improved by training, the implications would be enormous. First, we would have to adjust our thinking about human potential and the degree to which heredity and environment contribute to intelligence. But on a more practical level, school curricula could be specifically designed to produce better problem solvers, better thinkers, and generally smarter students who accomplish more in life. To think of the possibilities is exciting, but we're getting a bit ahead of ourselves because this research is only beginning. More research must be done before anything definitive can be said about the extent to which this type of specialized training affects intelligence.

Are We Already Getting Smarter? (The Flynn Effect)

What seems like a psychological oddity in the field of intelligence is the finding that IQ scores have been steadily increasing over the past 100 years. Political scientist James R. Flynn first reported this phenomenon in 1984. Since then, evidence has shown that these IQ gains, referred to as the *Flynn effect*, occur in many countries. Interestingly, though, there has been no corresponding increase in academic performance, suggesting that the increase may be due to something other than a genuine increase in intelligence. Some have speculated that the gains are due to improved nutrition, people becoming better educated, and society learning to use better strategies with timed tests, to name a few, but no one is really sure.

The Flynn effect could have relevance to your child. For example, if a student is being considered for a gifted program or other type of special education services, a difference of a few points could determine whether he or she is eligible for those services. If a recently released version of an IQ test is available, the psychologist will need to decide whether to use the newer version, which will reduce the Flynn effect and yield the most accurate scores, or the older version, which will give slightly higher scores. Ethically, though, whenever a new version of a test is published, professionals should start using it within a year of its release. The reason? A test is most valid right after it's released (because it's using updated norms) and least valid after several years of use (because it's using older norms).

Is There More Than One Type Of Intelligence?

So far, we've been speaking as though psychologists have identified only one type of intelligence—the type measured by traditional IQ tests. Can human mental abilities be so thoroughly explained by a single number called IQ? Have any new visions of intelligence been proposed in recent years?

Many theories of intelligence have been developed, but no particular theory is accepted by everyone. Perhaps the most persistent theory is one that suggests that our abilities are best explained by a single underlying intelligence. This is what psychologist Charles Spearman in the early 1900s referred to as "g," for general intelligence or general factor. Modern theorists, such as Howard Gardner and Robert J. Sternberg, view intelligence as multifaceted and believe the traditional concept is insufficient to explain the complexities of mental abilities.

The typical conception of intelligence, represented by the view that IQ is rigid and unchanging, has a historical advantage in our society that is not easily loosened from the grips of tradition, but Gardner and Sternberg's theories represent appealing alternatives. In his intriguing 1983 book, *Frames of Mind: The Theory of Multiple Intelligences*, Gardner proposed the idea that human abilities are actually represented by several types of intelligences. These include: 1) linguistic, 2) musical, 3) spatial, 4) logical-mathematical, 5) bodily-kinesthetic, 6) interpersonal, and 7) intrapersonal intelligence. Examples of how these relate to our everyday lives are listed in Table 10. As you look over these examples, consider how these intelligences might relate to your life and the lives of those you know.

Table 10

Gardner's View of Multiple Intelligences

Type of intelligence	What it involves
Linguistic	Use of language. *(Poet, writer, author.)*
Musical	Perceiving pitch/melody, rhythm & timbre of sounds. *(Musician, singer, composer.)*
Spatial	Visual perception of objects. *(Sculptor, architect, artist.)*
Logical-mathematical	Logical abstract thinking & reasoning skills. *(Mathematician, scientist.)*
Bodily-kinesthetic	Body movement. *(Dancer, choreographer, athlete.)*
Interpersonal	Understanding the behaviors & feelings of others. *(Psychologist, therapist, clergy.)*
Intrapersonal	Understanding your own behaviors & feelings. *(Philosopher, persons with keen self-awareness and insight.)*

It's certainly possible for an individual to possess a combination of these intelligences. For example, a scientist may possess both logical-mathematical intelligence and linguistic intelligence. Noted astronomer Carl Sagan comes to mind as a person representing this combination. He was a distinguished scientist yet was able to explain with elegant simplicity the wonders of the universe to people outside the scientific community and, ultimately, helped to make a difficult subject—astronomy—popular with the general public.

This list includes the seven original types of intelligences. Gardner (1999) later proposed two additional types—naturalist and existential. Examples of these are listed in Table 11. As research on multiple intelligences continues, it seems likely that the list will grow even more, again reminding us that human beings are more complex than previously thought.

Table 11

The Newer Intelligences Proposed By Gardner

Type of Intelligence	What it involves
Naturalist	Extensive understanding of nature. *(Biologist, botanist, horticulturist.)*
Existential	Understanding how one fits into the scheme of life and the universe. *(Philosopher, theologian, spiritual person.)*

Sternberg (1985) proposed his theory of "triarchic intelligence" as another challenge to the traditional notion of intelligence. (Triarchic simply means three.) According to this theory, three types of abilities—analytical, creative, and practical—make up intelligence.

Analytical abilities include making critical analyses, evaluating, and comparing and contrasting. Creative abilities consist of inventing, generating new ideas and theories, and discovering. Practical abilities are the "common sense" abilities and include things such as applying what you know to everyday living. Examples of how these three abilities might operate in everyday life include: Understanding and discussing the theory of how a car engine works (analytical ability) is different from inventing a new type of car engine (creative ability), which is different from being able to put an engine together (practical ability).

Sternberg (1997) sees these three abilities—analytical, creative, and practical—as being the basis for what he calls successful intelligence. He believes that successful intelligence is what really counts in life because it determines whether a person will be, well, successful. As Sternberg explains, though, success is more than simply having these three abilities; it's knowing when and how to use them.

Sternberg's idea of successful intelligence eventually could be a part of school testings to identify students for gifted and talented programs. Yale University researchers, for example, are investigating the usefulness of the Aurora Battery, a group of tests that utilizes successful intelligence concepts (Viadero, 2008). The test includes: a paper-and-pencil component that asks students to write a write a story or to generate a creative response to a scenario; a parent interview; a teacher's rating scale; and observation. The hope is that such a test will identify truly gifted and talented children missed by traditional IQ tests.

In a completely different vein, Daniel Goleman's 1995 bestseller, *Emotional Intelligence*, introduced the idea that emotions are important in our lives, perhaps even more important than IQ. The main idea behind emotional intelligence is that certain personal attributes and how we manage our emotions are important to success or failure in life. These are things such as self-disclosure, self-awareness, effective communication, decision-making skills, accepting personal responsibility, assertiveness, how we manage stress and conflict, insight, and social perceptiveness. This might help to explain those situations in life where individuals with very high IQs have bosses with excellent people skills but lower IQs, or why some individuals are so successful in life despite having unimpressive IQs.

More recently, Goleman (2006) proposed the idea that social intelligence also is important. He again de-emphasizes IQ and, instead, talks about our ability to connect to people at an interpersonal, or social, level. He suggests that virtually all interactions between people—from greeting a friend on the street to looking romantically into another's eyes or smiling when something good happens to a friend—not only touch our hearts but our brains as well. These social connections, both the good and the bad, Goleman says, affect our neural (brain) connections. We therefore must understand how biology and mood are related in order to make socially smart choices, choices that ultimately lead to a more satisfied life.

In different ways, Gardner, Sternberg, and Goleman's views reflect an appreciation for the complexities of human beings that cannot be explained by a single IQ score. Still, the traditional view of IQ is alive and well and continues to be well represented in the current crop of IQ tests. Parents and educators, therefore, should consider these traditional tests as good general measures but also must be aware that these tests may not tap all facets of human abilities.

A Comment on Genius

Before moving on to the next chapter, a comment on the topic of genius is in order. As we just learned, Gardner, Sternberg, and Goleman all suggest that other aspects to a person's life may be as important as IQ. Research on genius suggests something similar.

It's true that geniuses are usually intellectually bright, but millions of people have high IQs, and only an extremely small percentage of them will be thought of as true geniuses of the caliber of an Einstein, Da Vinci, Tesla, Edison, or Mozart. What sets geniuses apart from the rest of us still remains pretty much a mystery. Most experts do agree, though, that genius is not exclusively related to IQ. The reason for this is that genius is multivariate and results from an interplay of several factors, not simply IQ. In distilling the writings of some who've explored genius (e.g., Briggs, 2000; Csikszent-mihalyi, 1996; Howe, 1999; Sawyer, 2008; Shenk, 2010), some shared characteristics do emerge.

Aside from being bright, geniuses often show an obsessive focus in a specific area (e.g., science, math, physics, art, music), and they spend an inordinate amount of time exploring that interest. They tend to be driven, determined, exceptionally hard-working, curious, independent and inventive in their thinking, devoted to their ideas, and prolific generators of novel ideas. In the end, in almost all instances, they make significant positive contributions to their field and to the broader society, often impacting the global community.

With this in mind, parents and teachers should extend their efforts beyond nurturing a bright child's abilities and talents to also include encouraging critical thinking skills, curiosity, the expression of novel ideas, the taking of different perspectives, and other such attributes. Of course, there is no guarantee that this "whole child" approach will turn a bright child into a genius, but it almost certainly will benefit the child in whatever course he or she pursues in life.

CHAPTER 4

Proficiency and Achievement Tests

Few tests arouse as much concern and anxiety for students and parents as do proficiency tests, and for good reason. How well a child does during that week of proficiency testing can affect his or her entire life. Whether a child will be allowed to move to the next grade, receive an "honors" diploma, or graduate from high school could depend on their proficiency test scores. One thing is clear when it comes to proficiency tests...the stakes are high.

The climate in schools around proficiency test time is one of tension for students and parents, as well as for teachers, principals, and superintendents. The students, of course, are the ones who have to take the test and often are gently (and sometimes not so gently) pressured by parents and teachers to try their best. Parents obviously want their children to do well and nervously await the test results, hoping they will not have to explain to their child why he or she cannot be advanced to the next grade. It's not so surprising that many parents seem to be more stressed out by proficiency tests than their children.

Teachers, too, feel the pressure because they wonder if their skill and ability as an educator will be questioned if their students do not do well. And principals and superintendents anxiously await their "report cards" from the State Department of Education, informing them of how students in their schools fared. Their concern is whether parents, politicians, and state-level educators will see them as doing their jobs well. Sometimes they fear losing their job. And it's a fear based in reality. A 2003 story in the *The Plain Dealer*, a newspaper in Cleveland, Ohio, for example, told of four Cleveland-area principals whose contracts were not going to be renewed because of poor test scores at their schools (Reed, 2003).

A school that suffers from chronically low test scores could face an even more dire consequence—reconstitution. Reconstitution is when the entire staff at a school is removed and replaced with an all new staff. This sounds like an educational horror tale, but it's a reality that has occurred in various forms in several states (Stephens, 2008). Obviously, a lot is at stake—for students and educators.

What Are Proficiency and Achievement Tests?

Proficiency and achievement tests are fundamentally alike—both are designed to measure the knowledge or skills a child has learned in specific school subjects. For that reason, the terms proficiency test and achievement test are often used interchangeably. A test of math proficiency/achievement, for example, measures what a child has learned in math, and a test of science proficiency/achievement measures what a child has learned in science. The reason schools use proficiency or achievement tests, usually in the form of a standardized test, is to get an idea of how much a student has learned up to that point in time—to make sure he or she is making progress.

Although proficiency and achievement tests are basically alike, some differences do exist. Proficiency tests, for example, are administered exclusively in school settings. In contrast, achievement tests are used in a variety of settings, such as schools, mental health clinics, and private practices. Also, with proficiency tests, a standard (sometimes called a target or goal) usually must be met by the student; meeting this standard means the student is proficient, or competent, in the subject. With achievement tests, standards are not usually used. Instead, the results are simply reported as falling within a certain range (for example, average, above average, or below average).

Individual versus Group Testing

Another difference between proficiency and achievement tests is how they're administered. Proficiency tests are usually group-administered (but can be individually administered if necessary, for example, if a child was absent and needs to make up the test). Although some achievement tests can be administered either in groups or individually, the better ones usually require individual administration. Both approaches have their advantages.

The time, human resources, and cost benefits of using group-administered tests can be significant. A large number of children can be tested in a relatively short period of time, usually in only a few hours. And usually only one professional—the teacher—is needed to administer and supervise the test rather than a cadre of testing professionals whose time might be better spent with comprehensive evaluations. Overall, this translates into substantial savings for the school.

Individually administered achievement tests are used when a more detailed and comprehensive picture of a student's academic skills is needed. For example, a reading problem may have been detected from group testing, and the individually administered test often will be used as a follow-up to determine more clearly if a reading problem really exists and, if so, the type and extent of the problem.

Another advantage of individually administered achievement tests, and it's an important one, is that the examiner has an opportunity to establish rapport with the student. This was discussed earlier as it applies to individually administered IQ tests, and it also applies to individually administered achievement tests. Rapport is developed by taking time to chat with the child before beginning the testing with the intent of developing trust. This helps to put the student at ease so they can try their best. Also, with individually administered tests, the examiner usually has greater control over aspects of the environment, such as room temperature and noise level. And there's more opportunity to observe the child to see if he or she is ill, unfocused, or disinterested. This helps to explain why individually administered tests generally give more accurate results than group tests.

Classifications Based on Achievement Test Scores

A typical classification system for achievement test scores is provided in Table 12. (Keep in mind that although this is one of the most common systems used for achievement tests, it's not the only one.) The purpose of using a system like this, as mentioned previously, is to make scores more meaningful. For example, using this system, you easily can see that a score of 125 is above average and that a score of 86 is below average. Without a classification system, you wouldn't have any idea what a particular score means.

Table 12

Typical Classification System for Achievement Tests

Standard Score	Classification
130 and higher	Very Superior
120-129	Superior
110-119	High Average
90-109	Average
80-89	Low Average
70-79	Low
69 and lower	Very Low

You may have noticed that the standard score ranges are the same as those used with IQ tests (only the names of the ranges are slightly different). This is convenient for test users because it makes scores on IQ and achievement tests easier to compare.

Generally speaking, it's expected that a child's achievement standard score will be close to their IQ score. For example, if a student has an IQ of 100 (solidly average), it's expected that their achievement scores will be somewhere around 100. This, of course, does not always happen. Sometimes the achievement scores will be a lot lower than the IQ, or a lot higher. In either case, it's up to the psychologist or test expert to explain why a particular intelligence/achievement pattern occurred. Analyzing these patterns is important because they can provide valuable information about the reasons a student is having academic or learning problems.

Alternatives to Standardized Proficiency Testing

Standardized proficiency tests have been used in schools long before the federal *No Child Left Behind (NCLB)* legislation was signed into law in 2002. Even if *NCLB* is not reauthorized and fades into oblivion, standardized testing will almost certainly, in some form, be a major part of how our schools evaluate student progress.

Because the use of standardized tests is so deeply rooted in our educational system, it's hard to imagine there being alternatives, but there are. Their names may not have a familiar ring to them, but they are worthy contenders, if not as replacements for standardized proficiency tests, then certainly as complementary ways to evaluate student progress. Three popular alternatives include: 1) performance (authentic) assessment, 2) portfolio assessment, and 3) curriculum-based measurement.

Performance (Authentic) Assessment

The first alternative to proficiency testing that we'll discuss is called *performance assessment*, or *authentic assessment*. Performance assessment has been around for many years, but it's not widely used because it's been eclipsed by the popularity of standardized proficiency/achievement tests. But as criticism of standardized testing increases, and valid alternatives are offered, performance assessments are likely to get a fresh look.

Performance assessment requires students to demonstrate their knowledge through practical activities rather than by answering multiple choice or true/false questions. For example, in a performance assessment, a science lesson may require a student to construct a model of the solar system and to name and discuss the composition, mass, weight, and size of the planets and the relationship of the solar system to the universe. And for a geography lesson, the student may be required to plan a detailed trip around the world, stopping at the capitals of several countries and discussing the politics and culture of each country.

In each of these examples, the student would be graded against preestablished criteria, which are usually determined by the teacher. This is to ensure that a certain standard of quality is being met. As you can see, the strength of authentic assessment is that it reflects real-world learning rather than the sterile approach of multiple-choice and true-false exams. Moreover, it encourages *meaningful learning* rather than simple rote learning. And when learning is meaningful, children have more fun learning, learn more quickly, and most importantly, end up with a better understanding of the subject.

Portfolio Assessment

Portfolio assessment, like performance assessment, encourages genuine learning rather than the simple memorization of facts. With portfolio assessments, a student's classroom work is saved in a "portfolio," much like an artist or photographer saves their work. At the end of each grading period and at the end of the school year, the student's work is evaluated (using a scoring guide called a rubric) to see if progress has been made. The portfolio typically consists of an appropriate sampling of the student's work, carefully selected by the student and teacher; it is not simply a collection of random assignments tossed into a folder.

Unlike standardized tests where parents are presented with what can be confusing numbers, portfolio assessments allow parents and teachers to visually inspect and gauge a student's progress. For example, a parent can examine and compare stories written at the beginning of the year with those written toward the end of the year to see how their child's writing and thinking skills have developed.

Students also have a more active role in their learning. Portfolio assessment requires a dialogue, an exchange of ideas, between the student and teacher rather than expecting students to be passive receivers of information by sitting quietly and listening to a monologue from the teacher. They also learn the importance of cooperation while working on group projects, and most importantly, the very nature of the classroom discussions and activities encourages the development of critical thinking skills.

Curriculum-Based Measurement

The third alternative method of assessment that has generated a great deal of interest is called *curriculum-based measurement*, or *CBM*. Although CBM has been around for nearly 25 years, only recently has it emerged in schools as a viable alternative to the traditional and more time-consuming individual testing.

CBM is a quick and effective way to assess a student's skill levels in areas such as reading fluency, spelling, math, and written expression. Unlike traditional norm-referenced achievement tests, which usually take a considerable amount of time (often hours) to administer and score, administering a CBM is quick (usually 1 to 5 minutes) and scoring is straightforward. The child's score is compared to "benchmarks," which are determined from research and show what is "typical" performance in specific skill areas for children at different grade levels. Some advantages of CBM over traditional testing include:

- All students are screened; therefore, fewer students with learning problems are likely to fall through the cracks.

- Screening begins in kindergarten, so problems can be detected early in the child's schooling and interventions can be started early.

- They're quick and easy to administer and score using standardized procedures.

- They can be administered by teachers rather than by psychologists or other testing professionals whose time could be better spent with comprehensive evaluations.

- The focus is on providing appropriate instruction rather than on what is wrong with the child.

- The results are placed in a visual/graphic format, making it easy for parents and teachers to see a student's progress.

- The student can be given quick tests, called "probes," several times a week, so even a little progress can be measured.

- The content of the probes more closely matches what is actually being taught in the classroom.

- They are inexpensive and, therefore, highly cost-effective.

Although all of these advantages are important, perhaps the most important is CBM's ability to detect problems early enough to make a difference in a child's life. Early detection means early intervention, and ultimately, a greater likelihood that a child will be able to overcome deficits.

Issues in Proficiency and Achievement Testing

No type of testing is immune from criticism and controversy, and that includes proficiency/achievement testing. Some of the liveliest debates have centered on the issues of high-stakes testing, teaching to the test, using test scores as evidence of good teaching, using tests to measure whether standards are being met, and whether the pursuit of standards interferes with genuine learning. Let's take a short tour of these issues.

High-Stakes Testing

High-stakes testing is when a test is used to make a potentially life-altering decision. People often think of high-stakes testing as occurring only in school settings where standardized tests are used to make decisions such as whether a student should be promoted, retained, placed in a certain class, or allowed to graduate. But high-stakes testing is by no means limited to schools. Any situation in which a test is used to make important decisions rightly can be called high-stakes testing. Some states, for example, have laws prohibiting the execution of prisoners with an intellectual disability (mental retardation). Because an IQ test is one of the main instruments used to determine an intellectual disability, the score on this test will be a critical factor in deciding whether a person lives or dies. Indeed, high-stakes testing extends beyond the use of standardized tests in schools.

The potential impact of proficiency tests on the lives of school-age children was important enough for Congress to authorize the National Research Council (NRC), an arm of the prestigious National Academies, to investigate the use of high-stakes testing. The NRC study resulted in the 1999 publication, *High Stakes: Testing for Tracking, Promotion, and Graduation*, which outlined recommendations for appropriate test use by schools. Six of the eight recommendations are as relevant today as they were in 1999. They are briefly summarized here.

- Accountability for how well children perform in school is the responsibility of many groups and individuals—school personnel, politicians, parents, and students. In order to promote accountability, information about how to understand tests and test scores should be made available to the public as well as to school personnel and public officials.

- Before using tests to make high-stakes decisions, it is important that students first be taught the "knowledge and skills" that are on the test. In other words, what a student learns in class should be closely related to what is on the test.

- Test scores do not have to be used merely to make "either-or" decisions about a student, such as deciding to retain a child or not. Instead, test scores could point to a number of other ways of helping the student. For example, scores could be used to point to academic weaknesses, which would then be targeted for remediation.

- High-stakes decisions should not be made on the basis of a single score. Other sources of information related to a student's performance should be taken into account.

- It is improper to provide students with answers to a test or to present them with questions that will actually be on the test. But it is appropriate to "teach to the test" if the test covers what is in the curriculum (what students are being taught).

- Students with disabilities or English-language barriers could be negatively affected by standardized testing, but they should continue to be part of large-scale testing to track their progress and to make sure they're learning. The testing situation, however, should be modified to accommodate their disability.

These recommendations should be thought of as supplemental to the guidelines that already exist on the proper use of tests. One set of guidelines is the *Standards for Educational and Psychological Testing* (1999), developed jointly by the American Educational Research Association (AERA), the American Psychological Association (APA), and the National Council on Measurement in Education (NCME). The *Standards* is written for professionals and deals mainly with the technical issues of test development.

Another set of standards that is more easily digested is the *Code of Fair Testing Practices in Education*. The *Code* was written by the AERA, APA, and NCME, as well as the American Counseling Association (ACA), the American Speech-Language-Hearing Association (ASHA), the National Association of School Psychologists (NASP), and the National Association of Test Directors (NATD). Although the *Code* was written for testing professionals, it's also relevant to parents and teachers because it clearly describes what is meant by "fair testing practice."

According to Jay P. Heubert, a chapter contributor to *Raising Standards or Raising Barriers? Inequality and High-Stakes Testing in Public Education* (Heubert, 2001) and coeditor of the NRC High Stakes report, few educators and other test users seem to be aware that standards on the fair and appropriate use of tests even exist. Moreover, he contends that no strong enforcement mechanism is in place to ensure that the standards are being implemented. This is all rather startling in light of the widespread use of testing across all segments of society.

Information on how to obtain the *Standards for Educational and Psychological Testing* is available on the American Psychological Association's (APA) Web site (http://apa.org/). The *Code of Fair Testing Practices in Education* can be found at the APA Web site (http://www.apa.org/science/fairtestcode.html). And the NRC's *High Stakes: Testing for Tracking, Promotion, and Graduation* report can be found on the National Academy of Sciences' Web site (http://www.nas.edu/nrc/).

These publications are not only important resources for parents and teachers, but also for counselors, school administrators, policymakers, or anyone interested in the fair and appropriate use of tests. An awareness of what constitutes fair and appropriate test use by the very people who use tests, and especially by those whose lives are affected by them, is essential for creating a more effective system of checks and balances.

Teaching to the Test

Teaching to the test occurs when teachers focus primarily on the content areas known to be on a test. For example, if a teacher knows that the math section of previously administered standardized tests included many more addition problems than subtraction or multiplication problems, then teaching to the test would mean spending far more time (through practice, review, and drill) on addition and less time on subtraction or multiplication (even though all are important in life). Sometimes the practice, review, and drill are of old test questions, or clone-like questions that cover the same content areas as the real test. The goal, obviously, is to get high test scores, and in this age of educational accountability, test scores matter.

Teaching to the test is not when a teacher reviews with students the exact questions that will be on a standardized test. That's a form of blatant cheating, and there is no justifiable reason for this. Reviewing the format of the test also is not teaching to the test. In fact, making sure students are familiar with how the test is structured (e.g., multiple-choice questions, essay questions, short answer; what content areas are covered; the amount of time allowed for each section) or whether it's better to guess than to leave a question unanswered is considered to be a normal and acceptable part of the test preparation process.

Concerns that placing too much emphasis on standardized test scores will lead to teaching to the test have been voiced repeatedly, and they predate *NCLB*. A 1997 Associated Press story, for example, reported that the West Virginia Education Association had complained that "education administrators worry more about how students score on the tests than what they actually learn."

This sentiment still rings true, and it extends beyond the borders of West Virginia. A nationwide 2005 Phi Delta Kappa/Gallup Poll survey indicated that although 57% of the public supports the use of achievement tests, 58% believe the heavy emphasis on testing will cause teachers to teach to the test, which they consider to be negative (Rose & Gallup, 2005).

Opponents of teaching to the test argue that it forces teachers to focus only on those specific areas that will be on the test rather than other areas that also may be important. For example, we could end up not caring if students know the basic meaning of $e = mc^2$, who painted the Mona Lisa, or the events that led to Word War II if these are not going to be on the proficiency test. Or who cares if the biology teacher decides to skip the chapter on environmental science if this topic is not going to be tested?

McNeil and Valenzuela (2001) note other problems associated with teaching to the test. They cite that in Texas, for instance, where the Texas Assessment of Academic Skills (TAAS) testing program is used, many urban schools that serve predominantly African-American and Latino children have replaced traditional course time with time devoted to practicing for the TAAS, sometimes as much as several hours each week. These test drills for all intents and purposes have become part of the curriculum.

The result of all this drilling and practicing was rather surprising. According to McNeil and Valenzuela, this strategy did help to increase TAAS test scores for these students, but what the students learned was sometimes so fragmented that it did not generalize to real-life situations. For example, getting a passing score on the reading portion of the test did not necessarily mean that the students would be able to put these skills to practical use, such as being able to read a newspaper article. In other words, high test scores did not always mean that genuine learning occurred.

Could Teaching to the Test Be A Good Idea?

Teaching to the test often is regarded as something negative, but it's not difficult to find school administrators, teachers, and parents who consider it not only desirable but necessary for a quality education. From their perspective, teaching to the test offers some assurance that students are being taught the "right things." What are these "right things?" They're the standards that experts, usually at the State Department of Education, consider to be important.

Teaching to the test, though, may not be a bad idea in all circumstances. Whether it's a good or bad idea depends on which was developed first, the test or the curriculum. For example, if an off-the-shelf math achievement test is used to test students' knowledge in math, it's important that the test cover the types of math problems being taught in class. If not, the test and curriculum are said to have poor alignment. To compensate for this, some schools adjust their curriculum to make sure it covers what is on the test. If they didn't do this, test scores would suffer.

The problem with this approach is that the test dictates what is to be included in the curriculum. As we'll see shortly, *tests should be developed around curricula; curricula should not be developed around tests.* Also, some consider adjusting the curriculum to accommodate the test to be a dishonest practice because it promotes the idea that high scores reflect genuine learning (when that may not be the case).

A more appropriate type of teaching to the test is when the curriculum is designed first, based on clearly defined standards (as determined by educators and parents), and then tests are developed to measure those standards. This type of alignment is important because without it students could be learning a lot but it would not be reflected in the test scores (Goe, 2007). Another benefit of this approach is that it shifts the power of deciding what children should be learning from test makers to educators and parents. But perhaps most important is that it promotes genuine learning.

Despite the positive aspects of this type of teaching to the test, many still question the wisdom of allowing standardized tests to be the driving force behind our children's education. As we've already seen from McNeil and Valenzuela's research, in some instances teaching to the test may give us high scores but not necessarily useful, real-world skills. There may be other unintended consequences as well.

Impact on Critical Thinking

Critical thinking is a particular way of looking at the world and a way of solving problems. It involves asking probing questions and challenging accepted views, even those of experts. It means setting aside emotions and making rational decisions based on an analysis of the facts. A critical thinker is not merely a sponge soaking up and accumulating bits and pieces of information. Instead, they take in information, ask relevant questions, sort out what's important and what's not, and make decisions based on their analysis. Another name for critical thinker could be smart thinker. We want our children to be critical or smart thinkers because they'll accomplish more in life, will be less likely to have the wool pulled over their eyes, and will make smarter decisions.

It's hard to imagine that teaching to the test encourages critical thinking. Most standardized tests use multiple-choice formats where students have only a few minutes to come up with an answer. That's hardly enough time to apply critical thinking skills. For this reason, teaching to the test teaches students to solve standardized test problems, not complicated problems that require deliberative, critical thinking (Posner, 2004). In a similar vein, with all the testing required by *NCLB*, the climate in our schools has moved away from teaching critical thinking skills and nurturing intellectual engagement and toward teaching low-level skills as a means of preparing students for standardized tests (Solley, 2007).

The verdict is not in yet on whether teaching to the test stifles critical thinking. But because so much is at stake, wisdom should guide us to make sure that intellectual engagement and critical thinking are a normal part of classroom instruction.

Impact on Transformational Mentors

NCLB is a powerful law. Consider this: The amount of instructional time that schools devoted to reading and math since the passage of *NCLB* in 2002 has dramatically increased, whereas the amount of classroom time devoted to social studies, science, art, music, and physical education has decreased (Center on Education Policy, 2008). It should come as no surprise, then, that the two areas given the most instructional time—reading and math—were the areas targeted for testing by *NCLB*.

This increase in instructional time essentially means that teachers are teaching to the test for reading and math. But as mentioned above, teaching to the test is not always a bad idea. Another issue, though, is whether teaching to the test will have a more insidious effect by forcing teachers, especially the genuinely good ones, to alter their teaching styles.

Have you ever come across a teacher whose enthusiasm and passion for a subject and for teaching inspired you to learn? If so, then consider yourself fortunate; you probably had that special kind of teacher that Sternberg (2002) refers to as a *transformational mentor.*

According to Sternberg, transformational mentors are "the teachers and role models we never forget" (p. 68). They are the teachers who change lives in profound ways. They possess strengths that reach far beyond classroom competence, teacher certification, training, degrees, and even experience. They are able to recognize the strengths in a quiet, unpopular boy and are willing to take the time to draw out those strengths. They are able to believe in a failing student's capabilities when all others have given up. They are able to see and encourage the genuine talents of an overweight girl in dance class or the hidden gifts of a troubled youngster and show kindness, understanding, and acceptance when others have shown rejection. They are able to get one to believe in oneself. And perhaps most important, they nurture critical thinking and inspire their students to want to learn.

Will teaching to the test cause transformational mentors to become extinct? Will teaching to the test, which has increased considerably since the passage of *NCLB*, force these special teachers to become acquiescent, cookie-cutter teachers who produce acquiescent, cookie-cutter thinkers while leaving little time for the kind of enthusiastic teaching that inspires and fosters critical thinking? At this point in time, no one really knows.

What we do know is that a teacher's level of enthusiasm in the classroom can make a difference. A study by Patrick, Hisley, and Kempler (2000) for example, showed that when teachers were enthusiastic, students were more likely to be interested, energetic, curious, and excited about learning. Students also benefited when teachers showed an interest in students' social and emotional well-being, and when they offered challenging instruction and nurtured positive interpersonal relationships (Perry, Donohue, & Weinstein, 2007). For example, students had greater gains in math skills and more positive perceptions of their abilities; and a higher percentage of students met the standards in reading and math.

Just as we are unclear what impact teaching to the test will have on critical thinking, we are equally unclear what impact it will have on the teaching style of those special teachers who truly make a difference in children's lives. What is clear, though, is that our children deserve more of those types of teachers.

Test Scores as Evidence of Good Teaching

Tests have been around for a long time, and they've become an accepted part of the school culture. There is no massive public rejection of standardized testing, and no one disputes the obvious importance of accountability. As parents and educators, we want to make sure that our children are getting a good education, and we want proof. But what type of proof is best?

Some consider the results from standardized proficiency tests as the best way to hold teachers accountable. In other words, the scores students receive on these tests is "evidence" that teachers are doing their jobs well (or poorly), depending on how well (or poorly) their students do on the tests.

But believing that high test scores can reliably and accurately tell if a teacher is doing their job well requires a few assumptions. One is that all children across the country are equal in terms of family income, opportunities, home life, motivation, interests, emotional stability, life experiences, and the list goes on.

Students come to school with different maturational levels, different learning experiences, different cultural experiences, and different personalities. Some come from a "silver spoon" world where opportunities are abundant; others come from deplorable living conditions or home environments where parental disengagement, alcoholism, drug use, physical or emotional abuse, or neglect are the norm.

Another assumption is that all teachers are the same in terms of their level of enthusiasm, training and experience, teaching skills, expectations of students, willingness to help, and personality. And a third assumption is that all schools and classrooms are alike in terms of demographics (e.g., race, gender), class size, how the students interact with one another, climate of the classroom and school, engagement of parents, and quality and availability of teaching materials such as computers and updated textbooks.

If one thing is clear, it's this: Determining whether a teacher is doing a good job is a complex matter. All the things mentioned above can affect test results in significant ways, yet many are things that teachers have no control over. In light of this, a more reasonable approach would be to adopt better ways to hold teachers accountable than simply looking at students' test scores. What are these better ways? A starting point would be to consider some weighted combination of the students' grades, standardized test scores, and performance on different testing formats (e.g., portfolios, authentic testing) that reflect what actually is being taught in the classroom.

Using Tests to Measure Standards in Education

One particularly controversial topic has been the use of proficiency tests to measure standards in education. Standards are guidelines of what students are expected to know in school subjects such as math, science, and social studies. Standards usually are established by individual states and implemented at the local school district level. If a standard is met, let's say, in algebra, it is supposed to mean that the student has a reasonable understanding of algebra. In educational lingo, it means the student is proficient or competent in algebra.

A simple example of a standard would be something like this: All students must be able to read, at a minimum, at a tenth-grade level before being allowed to graduate from high school. Those who score at the tenth-grade level or higher on a standardized test will be allowed to graduate; those who don't can either retake the exam after more instruction, or they can choose to quit school.

It's hard to imagine anyone questioning the importance of standards in education. Without standards a child could end up with a hodgepodge of knowledge that has little bearing on their life. Worse yet, their education could be of such poor quality that they are unable to compete in college or in the workplace.

Standardized tests are the usual methods used to determine if standards are met. That seems to be reasonable enough. After all, there has to be some way to measure standards. Problems arise, though, when a single score or a rigid cutoff is used to determine if a standard has been met. Should a student be allowed to graduate if they missed the tenth-grade level by only one test question? Would it make a difference if that same student excels in math or science? What if a student misses the tenth-grade reading level by two points? Should they still not be allowed to graduate?

These types of situations really do happen, and they affect real people. One of the more disturbing stories is from several years ago and demonstrates the casualness, if not callousness, educational bureaucracies can show toward children's lives yet bow with reverence to tests. In a 1997 issue of *USA WEEKEND*, it was reported that an elementary school honor student who had earned several awards for academic accomplishments would not be permitted to graduate from elementary school (Ordovensky, 1997). The reason? She earned a 6.8 on the reading section of a standardized achievement test—the required passing score was 6.9!

Examples like this expose the weaknesses of using a single test or strict cutoff scores to make important decisions. It shows how tests are used to punish students rather than to help them. Test scores should be used along with other information, which could include classroom grades, teacher recommendations, observations, portfolios, performance assessments, and the student's past grades and accomplishments, or any combination of these. Using multiple measures leads to a fairer and more accurate appraisal of the child. And when considering that we are talking about our children's futures, it seems that the very least we can be is fair and accurate when making decisions that affect their lives.

CHAPTER 5

Personality Tests

People have a natural curiosity about themselves. The popularity of the so-called "personality tests" in fashion and glamour magazines attests to this. Some people believe that personality tests will reveal secrets buried deep within their psyche or perhaps even allow them to predict their future—much in the same way some people think of horoscopes. That is not likely to happen.

Personality tests may not be able to reveal our deepest and darkest secrets or predict our futures, but they can help us to understand what makes us tick. More specifically, personality tests are used for two fundamental purposes: 1) to help individuals learn more about themselves (for example, to foster personal growth and development), and 2) to determine whether emotional problems exist.

The personality tests that help individuals learn more about themselves are typically used with adults in career counseling situations, but they can be used in any situation where there's a need to assess "normal" behavior, such as in business settings. These tests measure characteristics such as introversion, extroversion, motivation, independence, interpersonal style, attitude toward work, and similar traits.

The personality tests that assess for emotional problems are used regularly in settings such as clinics, hospitals, private practices, schools, and mental health centers; and they can be used with children or adults. These tests measure things like anxiety, depression, impulsive behavior, unusual thinking, withdrawn behavior, and other types of thoughts, feelings, or behaviors. These tests can be particularly helpful in determining a diagnosis, measuring the severity of a problem, and evaluating progress.

What's important to remember when evaluating personality is that no one, child or adult, is perfectly emotionally healthy every day. Our lives are filled with emotionally sunny days and emotionally rainy days. Everyone is allowed to have some "wiggle room" in terms of problems and still be relatively "normal." Personality tests are designed with that in mind.

What Is Personality?

For our purposes, personality will be defined as a person's unique combination of traits, states, and types. These three elements of personality combine in such a way that allows us to distinguish one person from another in much greater detail than simply on the basis of physical attributes. Let's take a quick look at these traits, states, and types.

If you've ever described anyone as kind, warm, pleasant, introverted, shy, calm, short-tempered, aggressive, passive, outgoing, likable, honest, trustworthy, conscientious, and so on, you've described that person on the basis of their personality traits. Traits are personality characteristics that are stable over time and across settings. In other words, they're lasting characteristics. For example, if a person has a trait of being honest, we would expect this person to be honest today, tomorrow, next month, or next year. We also would expect them to be honest whether at home, at work, at the ballpark, or in any setting.

This stability of personality is particularly important because it helps us when making important decisions, such as when choosing friends or dating partners, and especially when deciding on a spouse. It allows us to really "know" a person. If people did not have personality traits, the only way to know someone would be on the basis of their physical features. Personality traits obviously play an important role in our lives.

Whereas traits are enduring personality characteristics, states are temporary ones. Honesty in the above example is a trait because it's more or less a permanent characteristic. But if a person becomes anxious only when he or she has to speak in public, this anxiety is considered to be a state because it's a short-lived condition that occurs only under certain circumstances.

The third aspect of personality, called types, is also important in personality assessment. Types are considered to be clusters of traits. Probably the most well-known types are the Type A and Type B personalities. For example, the traits of competitiveness, always being in a hurry, impatience, restlessness, and having a strong achievement orientation, cluster together to form the Type A personality. The opposite traits—calmness, patience, does not feel pressured to "beat the clock," and is not as driven by achievement or competition—collectively define the Type B personality.

Types of Personality Tests

Although several personality tests can be found in the psychologist's toolbox to measure states, traits, or types, they generally fall into two basic categories—objective tests and projective tests (also called projective techniques). Both approaches have the same general goal—to understand an individual better. The ways they reach that goal, though, are vastly different.

Objective Tests

Objective personality tests are especially popular with psychologists and educators. These tests use multiple-choice or true-false formats and are administered and scored according to very specific guidelines. An obvious advantage of this is that the scorer's biases, prejudices, and personal views do not affect the results.

Objective tests are also easy to administer and can be scored quickly and reliably. Although hand-scoring is still common and fairly quick, the increased use of computer scoring and interpretive software allows even quicker scoring without the risk of human error, with the added benefit of generating detailed test interpretations. Still another advantage of objective tests is that their predictions tend to be quite accurate, especially those that are generated by computer software that utilizes sophisticated statistical rules.

Among the most popular of the objective tests are the multidimensional ones. These are tests that measure several aspects of a child's personality. For example, a multidimensional test might include measures of depression, anxiety, somatic complaints (physical complaints), unusual thinking, hyperactivity, conduct problems (such as fighting, lying, and stealing), withdrawn behavior, and social introversion and extroversion—all in one test!

Despite the comprehensive nature of multidimensional personality tests, they cannot tell us every detail about or probe into every nook and cranny of a child's personality. No test can. People are just too complex. But these tests can be extremely useful because they cover many aspects of a child's personality or emotional functioning rather than just a single area. They also can be helpful in providing a general personality "picture," which we'll discuss in a moment.

Some objective personality tests measure only a single dimension of a child's personality. This type of test might measure depression only, hyperactivity only, or anxiety only. These tests also can be very useful, but they are somewhat limited because they measure only one dimension of a child's emotional functioning, and it's not uncommon for a child to be experiencing more than one problem at a time. To avoid this limitation, many psychologists will administer additional tests as a way of obtaining a more complete picture of the child's personality.

Projective Tests

Projective tests (also called projective techniques) are very different from the straightforward approach of objective tests. With objective tests the individual is usually asked to answer a series of questions in either a multiple-choice or true-false format. With projective tests the individual must respond to ambiguous stimuli, that is, to pictures or images that have no obvious meaning.

The popularity of projective tests is based on the belief that these techniques are capable of revealing thoughts and feelings at the deepest levels of personality—the subconscious and unconscious levels. If these deep levels can be tapped, so the reasoning goes, then that would allow the individual being evaluated to be understood more completely. Not every psychologist shares this view, though, as we'll see shortly.

The four basic projective tests used most often to evaluate children are: 1) the inkblot test, 2) picture cards, 3) picture drawings, and 3) sentence completion tests. These tests rarely are used alone but instead are usually part of a more comprehensive evaluation.

The Inkblot Test

The best known of the projective instruments is the Rorschach inkblot test. With the Rorschach, the psychologist shows the child a series of inkblots and then asks the child questions about what he or she saw. The child's verbal responses are written down in detail, scored, and then interpretations are made about the child's personality.

The child's responses to the inkblots are thought to be unconscious expressions of underlying personality dynamics. According to proponents of projective techniques, a major advantage of this indirect approach is that it allows the professional to tap into the child's unconscious mind, revealing deep-seated conflicts and motivations that otherwise would be unreachable.

Picture Cards

Another common projective test involves presenting a child a series of cards with each card showing animals or people in different scenes. The child is asked to respond to each card by describing what is happening in the scene and what the characters are thinking and feeling.

The appeal of this technique to some professionals is that the child's responses to the cards supposedly reveal information about need-based themes, such as a need for achievement, power, and intimacy. Additionally, their responses also may uncover anxieties and inner conflicts.

Drawing Pictures

A third common projective test involves having the child draw pictures. The picture could be of him or herself, of his or her family, or of a house, tree, or person. Some psychologists begin evaluations with a picture-drawing test because it's a non-threatening task that can help break the ice and ease the child into the more demanding parts of the evaluation.

The main reason picture-drawing tests are used is because the drawings are presumed to be symbolic representations of how the child perceives their self or family. Draw-a-person techniques sometimes are used to provide a very rough estimate of a child's level of intellectual functioning. Doing so, though, is inappropriate and unacceptable because far better tests designed specifically to measure children's intelligence are readily available.

Sentence Completion Tests

Sentence completion tests are yet another type of projective technique popular with some psychologists. With these tests, a child is presented with the first few words of an incomplete sentence (called the sentence stem) and is asked to complete the sentence. The following are examples (not real test items) of what part of a sentence completion test would look like.

I like sunny days _____.
When I go to school _____.
Books are _____.
When I am at home _____.

Sentence completion tests are used to obtain a general measure of a child's overall adjustment as well as to get information about the child's self-concept and attitudes. Like picture-drawing tests, sentence completion tests sometimes are given early in the evaluation process to help lower the child's anxieties before beginning the more challenging aspects of the evaluation.

How Personality Tests Are Administered

Personality tests can be administered in four basic ways: 1) self-report, 2) parent-report, 3) individually administered, and 4) group administered. Each format is briefly described.

Self-Report Tests

A common way to administer objective tests is to have the child complete the test. Tests administered in this manner are called *self-report* or *self-administered* tests. This is usually a paper-and-pencil test in the form of a true-false or multiple-choice questionnaire.

As mentioned earlier, many psychologists use special computer software to score these tests because doing so is much quicker and more reliable than hand scoring, and often a comprehensive computer-generated interpretive report is provided. This report, though, is usually not the final report but is more of a preliminary report. The final report will be tailored to the child and will include information obtained from a number of other sources, such as interviews with the child and family members, direct observation, as well as academic, developmental, behavioral, and medical histories.

A child must have basic reading skills (around the second-grade level) to complete a self-report test. In cases where the child is unable to read or has learning problems, such as a reading disability, a different format of the personality test may need to be given. For example, the child may be administered a tape-recorded version of the test, or the test questions may be read.

Parent-Report Tests

Some objective personality tests are designed to be completed by parents. These are not the same tests the child takes. Instead, they're specifically designed to be completed by a parent (or an adult who knows the child well) who answers questions, sometimes hundreds of short questions, about the child. These, too, are typically paper-and-pencil tests with a true-false or multiple-choice format, or they can be in a rating-scale format where the parent rates the child's behaviors from "never" to "very often."

The parent or person who completes this type of test, of course, must have sufficient reading skills, usually around the sixth to eighth-grade level, in order for the results to be valid. Not all adults know how to read. For those who have a reading disability or simply never learned how to read very well, this can be an embarrassing situation. The best thing to do is to discuss the situation with the psychologist or examiner, who will make necessary accommodations. Just as is done with the child who has poor reading skills, these accommodations could include using a tape-recorded version of the test or having someone read the test to the parent.

Individually and Group Administered Personality Tests

Administering a projective technique such as the Rorschach inkblot requires a one-to-one interaction between the child and the psychologist or examiner. Most projective techniques, in fact, can only be administered on an individual basis because they usually require that the examiner ask questions of the child and then accurately record in writing the child's responses. In contrast, objective tests that use a multiple choice or true-false format usually can be administered to either individuals or groups.

The amount of time it takes to complete a personality test, whether individually or group administered, varies greatly. Many behavioral rating scales are short and can be completed by parents or teachers in about 10 to

20 minutes. The more comprehensive objective personality tests, as well as many projective techniques such as the inkblot test, may take anywhere from one to two hours, or even longer, to complete.

What Does A Personality Look Like?

There obviously is no way to take a photograph of a personality. It would be nice to have a special "personality camera," but for now we'll have to leave such thinking to the realm of science fiction. Still, with many of the objective personality tests, such as true-false or multiple-choice personality tests, it is often possible to get a pretty good "snapshot" of an individual's personality. This "snapshot" is actually a graph, similar to the one in Figure 3.

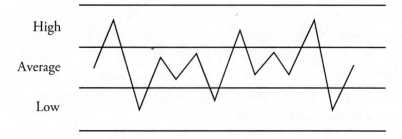

Figure 3. Example of what a personality might look like.

This graph can provide a surprising amount of detailed information to a trained professional. Of course, it can't reveal everything because humans are too complex, but still, the information it does provide is comprehensive and useful for developing a clinical picture of the child. Parents, teachers, and counselors, however, usually will not see this graphic profile. To an untrained person, this graph by itself will make little sense. If it is made available, a written statement or report will be attached and will include an interpretation of the results.

Beyond Personality Tests

Personality tests, like all tests, should not be used by themselves to make important decisions about a child. You may remember that the reason for this is that tests are not perfect; they all have some degree of measurement error, which is another way of saying they can be wrong. Even good tests have some amount of error and can be wrong some of the time. So in order to get a more accurate and complete portrait of a child's emotional functioning, it's important to go beyond test scores and use information from other sources, such as interviews and observations.

Interviews and observations are important because they provide a more direct glimpse than tests into the everyday life of a child. Interviews and observations show how the child is actually behaving—at home, at school, in restaurants, when visiting relatives, or while playing with friends? Is he or she sad much of the time? Does he or she fight a lot? Is sleep or appetite disrupted? Are there any irrational fears? And so on.

Because a child's parents often are the first to notice if something is wrong—a son's grades suddenly drop, he cries everyday, he becomes withdrawn, he loses interest in things he used to enjoy—they obviously are valuable sources of information. Teachers and other family members, such as grandparents, brothers and sisters, and aunts and uncles also may be able to provide useful information. Using interviews and observations in addition to personality tests provides a more detailed and accurate picture of a child's emotional functioning which, after all, is a primary goal of personality assessment.

Issues in Personality Testing

One of the big issues in personality testing is whether projective techniques are useful. If you think that this is nothing more than an academic discussion, it's not. As you'll see shortly, it's relevant to any parent whose child is evaluated with these tests.

Another issue in personality testing relates to labeling and stigmatization. Personality tests can reveal sensitive information which, if found out, could subject a child to ridicule, prejudice, or discrimination. We'll delve into that issue shortly. First, let's tackle the issue of the usefulness of projective techniques.

How Useful Are Projective Tests?

Projective techniques have their roots in psychoanalytic (Freudian) theory, and they have an almost mystical aura about them. Most people are simply amazed that so much can be learned about a person based merely on their responses to a bunch of inkblots, or by describing what they see in a series of pictures, or by the details they use when drawing a person or other objects. This seems to be due largely to projective techniques being portrayed in the media as psychology's "crystal ball," enabling professionals to reach into the deepest recesses of a person's mind. But can projective techniques really give us access to the far reaches of the mind? Can they help peel away our defenses and probe our deepest and darkest secrets?

Some professionals believe they can, but others have serious doubts about the usefulness of these tests. Lilienfeld, Wood, and Garb (2000), for example, conducted comprehensive analyses of three popular projective techniques—the Rorschach Inkblot Test, the Thematic Apperception Test, and human figures drawings. (With the Thematic Apperception Test, the examinee is asked to respond to a series of pictures.) Their analyses showed that the validity of these tests is so questionable that, "…it is virtually inevitable that the inferences routinely drawn from them by practitioners are often unjustified, erroneous, or both" (p. 53). That's a technical way of saying that when these tests are used, the results are likely to be wrong.

Garb, Wood, Lilienfeld, and Nezworski (2002) again looked at these three tests and basically came to the same conclusion—they all tend to over-predict emotional problems in children. In other words, these tests tend to predict the presence of emotional problems when none are actually present. That can lead to unnecessary diagnoses and treatment for the child and unnecessary anguish for the parents.

The implications of this research are far-reaching. Garb and his colleagues, for example, recommend that when evaluating children, psychologists should rely primarily on the child's history and on interview data from various sources rather than on the results of projective techniques. They also note that because of the limited accuracy of these techniques, it's best to stay away from using them to make important decisions, such as whether a child has been sexually or physically abused or whether a child should live with his mother or father following a divorce.

Not all professionals agree with Garb and his colleagues. In 1996, the American Psychological Association (APA) established the Psychological Assessment Work Group to investigate the effectiveness of psychological testing. Among the group's conclusions, which were published in the February 2001 issue of the *American Psychologist*, perhaps the most controversial was that "psychological test validity is comparable to medical test validity" (p. 128).

The Work Group also reported that projective techniques, such as the Rorschach and the Thematic Apperception Test "do not produce consistently lower validity coefficients than alternative personality tests" (p. 135). In other words, the results from projective tests are just as accurate as those from the objective, self-report types of personality tests.

Garb, Klein, and Grove (2002), however, challenged the credibility of the Work Group's findings. They even suggested that the Work Group's position may have been motivated by a desire to protect the testing practices of professional psychologists from further decline and from non-payment by managed-care companies.

In an apparent attempt to put this issue to rest, a 2005 statement by the Society for Personality Assessment in the *Journal of Personality Assessment* reported that the Rorschach is "validly similar to that of other generally accepted personality assessment instruments and its responsible use in personality assessment is appropriate and justified" (p. 219). Despite the confidence this statement reflects, it's unlikely to bridge the cavernous rift between testing professionals any time soon.

This arguing among professionals does little to instill confidence in parents about the tests being used to evaluate their children. If the experts can't agree, what can parents do? At the very least, they can ask questions. They should ask why a particular test is being administered, what it measures, if it's a good test, what makes it a good test, and how the results are to be used. In fact, parents should ask as many questions as necessary until they feel satisfied that their child is receiving the most accurate evaluation possible.

Do Personality Tests Label and Stigmatize Children?

It's no secret that society treats people with emotional disorders more harshly than those with more clearly defined medical problems, such as diabetes. For this reason, parents understandably are a bit wary when it comes to having their child tested for emotional difficulties. This type of testing, they fear, will label and stigmatize their son or daughter and make them vulnerable to what can be a cruel world.

Parents tend to view some tests as less threatening than others. They are so familiar with the school-wide proficiency tests their child takes in school, for example, that these tests do not set off any alarms; they're pretty much accepted as a normal part of school. Even IQ testing, once regarded as a particularly private matter, is generally considered a routine part of school evaluations nowadays.

Personality tests, though, are perceived differently, and for good reason. Questions on some objective tests can be very personal. A child might be asked about feelings of suicide, whether they worry about going crazy, or whether they've thought of running away. These are not matters a parent would normally want to share with anyone except trusted professionals or the closest family members.

Personality tests often bring out the curious and cautious side of parents. Parents are curious to know what may be troubling their son or daughter, but they also fear their son or daughter will be labeled (diagnosed with an emotional problem) and will forever be stigmatized as emotionally troubled or, worse yet, "crazy." Tests indeed are often used to help diagnose emotional problems. But diagnosing a child with, let's say, depression, also could mean that they will get needed treatment.

Stigmatization, though, is real. It reflects society's attitude toward mental illness. It's unlikely that stigmatization can be completely eliminated, but it can be greatly minimized. An initial step in this direction is for professionals to use only scientifically sound tests when evaluating children in order to avoid incorrectly interpreting results that could lead to wrong and unnecessary diagnoses.

Another step is for professionals who conduct testings or evaluations to keep all results and any information gathered for the evaluation strictly confidential. Being assured that their child's testing results will be held in the strictest confidence often can ease a parent's fears and worries. Parents can take some comfort in knowing that virtually all mental health and health professionals already do this. The reason is that it's considered a standard in ethical practice that's taken very seriously.

School personnel also must understand the sensitive nature of testing and the importance of keeping results confidential. Casually discussing test findings over a cup of coffee in the teacher's lounge with those who do not have a clear need to know can have unintended consequences. It could change a teacher's perception of a student and affect how that child is treated in the classroom.

What may seem like harmless hallway conversations between teachers also can be risky. Words overheard by students could inadvertently create targets in the schoolyard, where terms such as "dumb," "stupid," or "crazy" are aimed at classmates. Even if said lightheartedly, these words can be damaging and hurtful. Tragically, some children will take these words to heart and will end up believing things about themselves that are not true.

Everyone has a role to play in curbing stigmatization. Parents, teachers, and school administrators need to become better educated about common childhood emotional disorders in order to separate fact from myth. Also, teachers and administrators need to actively promote an atmosphere of acceptance in their classrooms and schools, whether it's through classroom readings and discussion, formal lesson plans, or community advocacy. Without these kinds of fundamental changes, there is little reason to expect change to occur beyond a snail's pace.

CHAPTER 6

College Admissions Tests and Career Interest Inventories

Parents want the best for their children. They want their children to be successful, to live life to its fullest, and to be happy. The road to success, fulfillment, and happiness requires having clear goals and clear directions for reaching those goals. Life is far too precious to make choices in an aimless, flip-of-the-coin manner. But before beginning the journey to their dreams, millions of high school juniors and seniors must face one final hurdle—the college admissions test.

Career interest inventories (sometimes called vocational interest inventories) are used to help individuals answer the question, "What should I do with my life?" Choosing a career is certainly more complicated than filling out a career inventory, but these inventories can help students select a college major well suited to their interests that hopefully will lead to a satisfying career. Some people know exactly the career they want to pursue, but many do not. Career interest inventories can be particularly helpful for this latter group.

Before considering college majors and careers, though, students first must successfully navigate the college admissions process, which includes taking the SAT or ACT. These tests have become a rite of passage into the world of higher education for millions of high school students. The pressure to get the highest possible scores can be intense. How a student performs on these tests can determine whether they set sail for one of the best colleges in the country or one they consider to be further down the ladder of prestige.

College Admissions Tests

College admissions tests have received their share of criticism over the years, being called everything from "scams" to the more kindly "necessary yardstick." Whatever one's view, the fact remains that college admissions tests are deeply embedded in the American psyche, and they are not likely to be whisked away into he dustbins of history any time soon. In fact, according to the College Board Web site, slightly more two million students take the SAT each year; and according to an ACT press release, a record 1.42 million students took the ACT in 2008.

The SAT and ACT are given to high school students during their junior or senior years to help determine whether they can handle the rigors of college. The SAT is considered to focus on reasoning and problem-solving skills, whereas the ACT is said to be more directly related to the actual coursework during high school, such as English, math, reading, and science.

You should know that the SAT mentioned here refers to the SAT Reasoning Test or what used to be called the SAT I. Generally, whenever someone refers to the SAT, they mean the SAT Reasoning Test. There is another kind of SAT—the SAT Subject Test—which measures knowledge in specific subject areas (English, science, various languages, and mathematics). The SAT Subject Tests used to be called the SAT II: Subject Tests.

A claimed advantage of these nationally standardized college entrance tests is that they provide a standard that colleges and universities can use to compare high school students with different backgrounds. The SAT or ACT scores of a high school student in Oregon, for example, can be compared to the scores of a high school student in Maryland, even though the two may have taken different courses or come from different cultural backgrounds.

Many colleges and universities have established a range of scores on these tests that they consider to be acceptable for the student seeking admission. In general, students with high test scores and high grade point averages (GPA) have a better chance of getting into the more selective colleges or universities than students without this combination. Class rank, difficulty of curriculum (such as taking honors classes or Advanced Placement classes), extracurricular activities (such as being a member of school and community organizations, participating in sports, doing volunteer community service, or heading up or participating in local fund raisers), and teacher or counselor recommendations also may be important elements in the admission process.

All elements of the admission process are not given equal importance. It's entirely possible that a person with a high GPA but average test scores could be knocked out of the running for admission to a competitive college. The opposite pattern, where the student has high test scores but an average GPA, also can remove a student from consideration and may even be viewed more unfavorably because the GPA is generally considered to reflect the student's motivation. In general, GPA and test scores are regarded as the most important factors, or at the very least screening "starting points," among the most selective colleges, but each school weighs the factors differently.

The Baby SAT?

A test sometimes confused with the SAT is the Preliminary SAT (PSAT), or what some call the "baby SAT." The PSAT is similar to the SAT but shorter, and as the word "preliminary" suggests, it often is considered to be practice for the SAT. Unlike the SAT, though, the PSAT is not a college entrance test. A better name would be the "scholarship eligibility test." In fact, on the College Board Web site (http://www.collegeboard.com/student/testing/psat/about.html), this test is formally referred to as the Preliminary SAT/National Merit Scholarship Qualifying Test (PSAT/NMSQT) and is co-sponsored by the College Board and National Merit Scholarship Corporation.

The PSAT/NMSQT measures critical reading, math, and writing skills and is generally given to students in their junior year of high school. The National Merit Scholarship provides college scholarships for thousands of students entering undergraduate training.

Issues in College Admissions Testing

College admissions testing, like its distant cousins intelligence, proficiency, and personality testing, has plenty of controversy swirling around it. The most heated issues relate directly to their usefulness in the admissions process. These include whether they truly represent a "standard" by which students of different backgrounds can be compared, whether coaching can improve scores to any substantial degree, and whether they really are needed in order to correct for grade inflation.

Usefulness of College Admissions Tests

College admissions tests can be relatively good predictors of success in the first year of college, but are they the best predictors? In *None of the Above: The Truth Behind the SATs* (1999), David Owen and Marilyn Doerr argue

105

that using the SAT does not contribute substantially to the prediction of college success. High school grades, they note, generally are as good if not better predictors. They point out that if colleges were to stop using the SAT altogether, the consequences would not be as tragic as some believe and, in fact, the admissions process might actually improve. Colleges could then dedicate more time to the truly substantive issues, such as the student's GPA and whether the student took rigorous courses in high school, rather than be distracted by the student's SAT scores.

Peter Sacks, author of *Standardized Minds* (1999), also argues against using the SAT. He points out that the SAT adds so little to the prediction of success in college that to continue using it in the college admission process is highly questionable.

This view may be getting some traction. In the October 3, 2007 issue of *Education Week*, it was reported that a special 20-member commission of the National Association for College Admission Counseling met to discuss the usefulness of admissions tests (Cech, 2007). One of the suggestions was to make these tests optional rather than required in the college admissions process. This is already happening at some schools. According to 2009 data from the National Center for Fair & Open Testing (FairTest), a watchdog and advocacy organization, more than 800 colleges and universities already have either eliminated, de-emphasized, or allow more flexible use of SAT or ACT scores in the college admission process.

Still, there are more than 2000 four-year colleges and universities in the United States. Why, then, do the majority of these schools continue to require either the SAT or ACT? Sacks (1999) offers one explanation. He suggests that America is "a country obsessed by numerical rankings as the measure of quality" and, therefore, we have come to expect that numbers provide the only way to measure quality.

In his book, *The Mismeasure of Man* (1996), scientist Stephen Jay Gould addresses this very point. For example, he talks about a trend among the social sciences that began in the second half of the nineteenth century, a trend he refers to as the "allure of numbers." This was a false belief that the use of numbers allowed human characteristics to be measured with such accuracy that the social sciences could be viewed as scientifically precise as physics. But it may be more than the simple "allure of numbers" that explains the continued use of college admissions tests.

Sacks (1999) suggests that some colleges and universities may be motivated to use college entrance test scores to create a prestigious image—those that accept students with the highest scores can claim to be more prestigious and selective than those accepting students with lower scores. And Owen and Doerr (1999) note that many colleges, even those that have open-admission policies, require SAT scores to give the appearance of being selective.

Another reason for the continued use of the SAT and ACT may be related to the unyielding nature of our belief system. After so many years of using these tests, it seems we've come to believe that they must be useful, even when the evidence may be unconvincing. Because beliefs are highly resistant to change, it may be quite some time before college and university gatekeepers decide what changes, if any, need to be made to the role of these tests in the admissions process.

Despite widespread criticism leveled at college admissions tests, some researchers (e.g., Sackett, Borneman, & Connelly, 2008) have conducted comprehensive analyses of these tests and found them to be fairly good predictors of success in college. That in itself may be sufficiently convincing to college administrators to continue using these tests. Still, the amount of conflicting evidence on the usefulness of college admissions tests is abundant and only adds to the confusion regarding their validity, especially to students and parents. Moreover, although they may be good predictors of college success, there is scant evidence that they are substantially better than other predictors, such as GPA.

Can We Have High Standards Without Tests?

One of the most common arguments for using the SAT or ACT in college admissions is that they provide a "common yardstick" or "standard" by which applicants of different backgrounds can be compared. But would colleges be able to select quality students without using this standard?

In an article published in *University Business* in 2004, well-known educational consultants Howard Greene and Matthew Greene point out that highly selective and competitive schools that do not use SAT or ACT scores continue to maintain a standard of excellence. As an example, they cite a study by Bates College, a private college in Maine with a history of being among the elite of small liberal arts colleges. The study looked at a 20-year period during which Bates College gave incoming students the option of submitting their SAT scores. The results showed no significant difference in academic performance and graduation rates between students who submitted SAT scores and those who did not.

Another example is Mount Holyoke College, a small, private, top-tier liberal arts college in Massachusetts. In 2001, Mount Holyoke College changed their admissions policy and made submission of standardized test scores optional. As stated on their Web site, rather than relying on standardized test scores, they expanded the admission criteria to include the student's high school record, essays, and a graded paper from high school. The admission committee also made an effort to determine a prospective student's level of "intellectual curiosity, motivation, leadership, creativity, and a social conscience." Analysis of preliminary data showed that the first class to be admitted under the new policy, the class of 2005, was not only as academically capable as students from earlier classes, but also more diverse.

In 2006, a several-year study supported by a grant from the Mellon Foundation found no significant difference in GPA between Mount Holyoke students who submitted SAT scores and those who did not. In fact, the study revealed that the collective GPA difference between these two groups was a mere one-tenth of a point.

Does Test Coaching Help?

Considering the abundance of test preparation courses available to students, it's only logical to wonder whether college admission tests are being contaminated by test coaching, resulting in score inflation. Each year tens of thousands of students are involved in some form of SAT or ACT coaching. It may be from formal test preparation programs costing several hundreds of dollars, from courses offered as part of the high school curriculum, or from private tutors. Add to this the various Internet sites offering advice and practice tests. And some students will do it on their own by purchasing a test preparation study guide at the local bookstore.

With so many types of coaching available, from the simple to the elaborate, there is no accurate way to determine who has received coaching and to what degree they may have benefited. As a result, admission committees never really know if the score in front of them is a "true" score or an inflated score due to coaching. That would seem to weaken the argument that the SAT is a "standard" against which all applicants can be judged.

But not everyone agrees that test coaching helps. For example, Richard P. Phelps, in his book, *Kill the Messenger: The War on Standardized Testing* (2003), cites a number of studies that show test-coaching courses are not particularly effective. He notes that if any gains are made, they are likely to be small.

In *Rethinking the SAT* (2004), Derek C. Briggs reported that gains from commercial coaching programs generally are between 3 and 20 points for the SAT verbal portion, and between 10 to 28 points for the SAT math portion. That's not enough to make much of a difference in college admission decisions. Others (e.g., Sackett, Borneman, & Connelly, 2009) have reported that coaching may produce some increase in scores, but the gains are generally much smaller than what is claimed by test preparation companies.

The saga does not end here. Claims about the benefits of test preparation courses abound and vary so greatly that it's difficult for parents to judge whether these courses help in any meaningful way. In an issue of the *American School Board Journal*, for example, it was reported that a 17-year-old was able to raise his SAT score 400 points after three attempts at the test (Black, 2005). And companies that offer test preparation courses, citing their own studies, generally claim gains of around 100 points, and sometimes as much as 200 points. These differences are large and could sway a decision at a top-tier college their way.

Because so many college-bound students are "prepping" for these tests, parents often feel it's necessary for their own son or daughter to take a preparation course in order to keep up with the competition. And because the competition is sometimes so fierce, some students begin preparing for these tests as early as their middle school years.

Parents must believe that coaching helps at least somewhat. As a group they are spending millions of dollars each year on test preparation courses for their sons and daughters. These courses can be helpful to the extent that they familiarize students with the test, provide an opportunity to take practice tests under the same conditions as the actual test, and provide an opportunity to develop effective test-taking strategies. Moreover, the very process of preparing for the test may result in some genuine learning.

On the downside is that many students cannot afford expensive test preparation courses. (Classroom SAT preparation courses offered by private companies, for example, can range anywhere from $500 to over $1000.) These students could be at a disadvantage in the highly competitive race of applying to and getting into a top-ranked college. After all, they will be competing with the tens of thousands of students who have taken test preparation courses. But parents can do things to reduce this disadvantage.

- Some high schools offer test preparation programs either as part of the curriculum or as extracurricular courses. If your child's school offers such a program, encourage him or her to enroll in it.

- If you have a computer at home, consider purchasing test preparation software. This software is available at most office supply stores and at various online software stores for under $50,.

- If your son or daughter has access to a computer, he or she can connect to test publishers' Web sites as well as private Web sites that offer an abundance of useful information about college entrance tests. This includes sample questions, "tips and tricks," and even practice tests that can be taken on the computer while surrounded by the comforts of home.

- If your child does not have access to a computer, don't lose hope. A great resource located in most communities is the public library, which usually has computers with Internet access available to anyone with a current library card.

Because so much is available to help students prepare for college entrance exams, combined with convincing advertising claims, it's easy to end up thinking that taking a test preparation course will guarantee a higher score. It's not that simple. There's a good chance that taking such a course will help, but the degree to which it will help remains debatable.

Many experts believe that the best test-taking strategy is to have students develop effective work habits early in their education—by studying, being diligent about completing homework, taking challenging courses—and continuing this throughout their school years. Even this approach may not lead to particularly high test scores, but the chances are good that it will result in something far more important, more useful, and more valuable to the student in the long run—a good education.

The Facts About Grade Inflation

Grade inflation is when teachers give students higher grades than they actually deserve. This "inflation" of grades is why some say that standardized tests such as the SAT and ACT are more accurate indicators of a student's progress than grades and, therefore, should be given more weight in the admissions process. Grade inflation is believed to be a problem in high schools and colleges across the country, but is it really as much of a problem as some claim?

The whole concept of grade inflation is interesting and confusing. As a nation, we push our children to do better in school, and when they do better, we say that shouldn't happen and call it grade inflation. In other situations, we see grade point averages go up but with no corresponding increase in SAT or ACT scores, and then say this is evidence of grade inflation, for some reason believing that college admission test scores are the gold standard against which grades should be judged.

In a 2002 issue of *Chronicle of Higher Education*, educational activist Alfie Kohn referred to grade inflation as a "dangerous myth" and cited research indicating that grades actually have declined from around the mid 1970s to the mid 1990s. Others, such as George D. Kuh and Shouping Hu, in an article published in a 1999 issue of *Educational Evaluation and Policy Analysis*, report that grade inflation tends to be more common at research universities and selective liberal arts colleges than at colleges in general. Interesting is that they also found evidence of an opposite trend—*grade deflation*—occurring at other types of colleges and universities.

What is grade deflation? It's when a teacher makes a course so difficult that it's almost impossible for a student to receive an A. Another example is when a teacher structures the grading system so that only a certain percentage of students will receive As, a certain percentage will receive Bs, and so on, even though the performance levels of the students might be close to one another. Unlike grade inflation, grade deflation is rarely discussed by the educational community because it's usually not thought of as a problem.

What is particularly noteworthy about the Kuh and Hu (1999) study is that they found that higher grades across all types of schools generally were associated with a student's academic effort. In other words, the reason students are getting better grades is because they're working harder.

Maybe it's simply a matter of a cynical society finding it hard to believe that students are getting somewhat higher grade point averages because they are working harder. But it's very real that students are under immense pressure to do well, either to pass a proficiency test or a graduation exam, not to mention the intense competition to get into graduate and professional schools. With so many pressures to achieve, hard work is a reasonable explanation for students doing better in school.

When looking at grade inflation with a critical eye, evidence supporting it is not as convincing as some might have us believe. An excellent summary of findings can be found in a 2004 issue of the *Association for the Study of Higher Education—Education Resources Information Center (ASHE-ERIC) Higher Education Report* titled "Reexamining the Empirical Evidence." According to this report, "Most of the increase in college grades appears to be the result of factors other than grade inflation. In fact, no systematic evidence supports the assertion that grade inflation is widespread" (p. 42).

Career Interest Inventories

If parents were asked if they would like their son or daughter to choose a career best suited for him or her and at the same time possibly save thousands of dollars down the road, the answer almost certainly would be a resounding yes. How can this be done? By having their 17 or 18-year-old receive effective career guidance before deciding on a college major or making a career choice.

The cost of a college education can range anywhere from a few thousand dollars a year to over $50,000 a year when taking into account tuition, textbooks, room and board, and the many miscellaneous expenses a student will encounter.

A college education is a worthwhile but expensive investment, and making a well-informed career choice could save thousands of dollars in retraining costs down the road.

Choosing a Career

Take a moment to reflect on how you chose your career. Did your parents encourage you to follow in their footsteps? Did your friends influence you? Was the amount of money you could make a strong consideration? These are some of the most common reasons people give for choosing a career, and often they're not the best reasons, especially if the ultimate goal is to find a career that will be satisfying. Without proper career planning, your chances of spending a third of your life doing something you don't enjoy increases… and so does your risk of unhappiness.

Choosing a career is one of the most important decisions a person will have to make in life. Thousands upon thousands of individuals are unhappy in their careers. They include physicians, lawyers, secretaries, social workers, mechanics, electricians, teachers, assembly line workers, salespersons, store managers, plumbers, business executives, and the list goes on. With so much at stake, it's surprising that most people put so little time and effort into choosing their life's work.

Research has shown that individuals will be happier and find their work much more satisfying if they are in a career they genuinely like. Good career guidance can remove a great deal of the guessing or trial-and-error from making a career choice and can help save considerable time and money and spare you years of both job and personal dissatisfaction.

Although many tools can be used in the career counseling process, the use of career interest inventories is a fundamental aspect of this process. These inventories generally are given to individuals at a stage in their lives when they are beginning to seriously consider what they would like to do with their lives. So, you are likely to see interest inventories used extensively during the late high school years and into early adulthood.

Interest inventories also are used with older adults. Many older individuals want a career change because they are bored or extremely unhappy with their careers. For others, it may be because they lost their jobs through company downsizing or layoffs. In such cases, the use of career interest inventories is an important element in the broader guidance process than can help a person find a satisfying career.

Some basic interest inventories are given to junior high and middle school students. At this age, though, career interests are usually not fully developed and are likely to change down the road, so you'll want to be careful about prodding a child into a particular career choice based on these early results. Of course, some students know from an early age exactly what career path they want to follow, but that is more the exception than the rule. For most youngsters, the value of using interest inventories at this young age is simply to get them to think about and to explore the many different careers available, not to decide on a career.

What Do Career Inventories Measure?

The use of career interest inventories plays an important role in helping people choose a career that's best suited for them. These tests measure career interests. More specifically, they measure how similar or dissimilar a person's interests are to the interests of successful persons in various occupations—nothing more. For example, if an individual has a high score in the occupation of computer programmer, it simply means that his or her interests are *similar* to the interests of computer programmers and that he or she probably would enjoy this type of career. If they receive a low score in the occupation of computer programmer, then it means their interests are *dissimilar* to those of computer programmers and they probably would not find this work enjoyable.

Some people confuse a high score on a career interest inventory with high ability, but career interests and abilities are two distinct areas. In other words, *career interest inventories measure career interests, not abilities.* Therefore, a high score in certain career areas of a career interest inventory simply means the individual has a high interest in those areas, not high ability. A person, of course, must also have the abilities to pursue a particular career, but those abilities are assessed with other instruments, such as intelligence or aptitude tests, not with career interest inventories.

Steering Your Son or Daughter
in the Right Direction

In order for parents to help their son or daughter choose a career, it's important to understand that their career interests may not be fully formed until late adolescence or early adulthood and, for some, even later. Every year thousands of college freshmen and sophomores change their major, either because their interests were not clearly developed or because they received inadequate career guidance, or none at all.

The quality of career guidance services offered by high schools varies greatly. At one extreme are schools that do everything possible to help a student make good career choices. Counselors at these schools may meet with students individually to review results of career testing. Some may meet regularly to discuss selecting a college major and the pros and cons of attending a particular school. Many counselors have a wealth of detailed knowledge about what specific colleges are looking for in a student and will try to match the student to the right college. If a student is not college-bound, the counselor may help by guiding them to an appropriate vocational program or an on-the-job training program that he or she will find gratifying.

At the other extreme are schools that do not place much emphasis on career guidance other than giving students a career interest inventory to complete and later handing them a computer printout of the results. That's not very effective guidance, but it happens a lot. That's unfortunate because deciding on a career for many will be one of the most important decisions of their life. It should be based on genuine career interests and careful career guidance, not on passing fads or fleeting interests.

Parents also may want to consider the services of a professional career counselor. These counselors often can be found in the phone book, but it's a good idea to ask around for references in order to find someone who provides top-notch services. Professional career counselors, of course, charge for their services, and sometimes their fees can be hefty. Some parents claim they're worth every penny. Still, don't overlook your child's high school as a resource. You may discover that your son or daughter's high school has talented and dedicated counselors who are eager to help.

If your son or daughter is a college student and is having difficulty deciding on a major or a career, direct them to the student counseling center. Most colleges have counseling/career centers staffed by professionals who can provide career interest inventories in addition to more comprehensive guidance services, and there's no charge. For those who are job hunting, visit your local library or bookstore and check out the hugely popular *What Color Is Your Parachute?* by Richard Nelson Bolles. It's published annually, and it's loaded with helpful career and job-seeking information.

CHAPTER 7

Other Useful Tests

Intelligence tests, achievement tests, and personality tests are the heavyweights of tests. They are the main tools in the psychologist's testing toolkit. But human beings are complex creatures, and sometimes other tests are needed in order to form a more complete picture of the individual, to understand a problem better, or to help with making an accurate diagnosis. And, for simple screenings, the "big guns" may not be needed at all

D eciding which tests to administer to a child is guided by the reason the child is being referred. For example, a child referred because of a suspected learning disability will be administered different tests than one referred for a behavior problem. Aside from the "big three"—intelligence, achievement, and personality tests—several other types of tests are worth mentioning because they, too, often are used in the evaluation process. These include school readiness tests, adaptive behavior scales, visual-motor tests, rating scales, neuropsychological tests, and tests used to evaluate children with disabilities.

School Readiness Tests

Playing with blocks, identifying basic shapes, learning colors, singing the alphabet, building clay models, and waiting for story time are all part of the preschool scene. But what you may not know is that many schools also require that students entering kindergarten or first grade be evaluated with readiness tests.

The purpose of readiness tests is to assess a child's skill levels when they begin school. By doing this, teachers will be able to teach to the child's unique skills and abilities and, if necessary, remediate any weaknesses. Parents, of course, worry that readiness tests will be used to exclude their child from school. Readiness tests, though, should not be used for that purpose because they are not always good predictors of school success. Children at this young age are going through rapid developmental changes, so even a couple of months of growth could result in substantial changes in test scores. Readiness tests also should not be used to make placement decisions, or any important decision. Those decisions are best made with a comprehensive evaluation.

Many professionals feel that the best basis for determining whether a child should attend school is the child's chronological age, not test scores. In other words, if a child meets the school district's age requirement for school entrance, then they should enter school. That makes sense. What wouldn't make sense would be to keep a child from the very things that would nourish their development—all the rich academic and social experiences that school has to offer.

Adaptive Behavior Scales

The main use of adaptive behavior scales is to evaluate individuals with an intellectual disability (mental retardation). You may remember from Chapter 3 that in order to diagnose an individual with an intellectual disability, he or she must be significantly below average in terms of intelligence and adaptive behavior functioning; and these must occur before the age of 18. Intellectual functioning is assessed with individually administered IQ tests, and adaptive behavior is assessed with adaptive behavior scales.

Adaptive behavior scales measure self-help/independent living skills. These are skills needed to care for oneself on a day-to-day basis. In 2002, the American Association on Mental Retardation (renamed the American Association on Intellectual and Developmental Disabilities in 2007) refined their definition of adaptive behavior to include "conceptual, social, and practical skills." You may recall from Chapter 3 that examples of *conceptual skills* include expressing oneself, understanding others, reading and writing, making decisions for oneself, and dealing with money; *social skills* examples include interacting with people, understanding potential hazards and threats, following rules, and obeying laws; and examples of *practical skills* include toileting, dressing and feeding oneself, using transportation, housekeeping skills, and work skills.

Adaptive behavior scales also can be helpful when evaluating persons suspected of having a pervasive developmental disorder, such as Asperger's disorder. The cardinal symptom of a person with Asperger's disorder is a substantial deficit in social or interpersonal skills, which is an area normally measured by adaptive behavior scales.

Visual-Motor Tests

Visual-motor tests measure eye-hand coordination and perception. (Perception is recognizing and interpreting an object that you see. For example, you might recognize the letter "b" and interpret it accurately as a "b," or inaccurately as a "d"). These are skills a person uses when putting puzzles together, building with blocks, or writing and drawing. With these types of activities, the child uses his or her hands and eyes, which must be able to work together in a coordinated manner. These skills also can affect subjects such as reading. For example, if a child is perceiving (i.e., recognizing and interpreting) letters incorrectly, it's likely that he or she will have difficult reading words with those letters.

Visual-motor tests usually require the child to copy geometric designs that gradually increase in complexity. For example, a six-year-old may be asked to draw a vertical line, then a circle, then a square, then a triangle, then a diamond, all the way up to three-dimensional figures. The child's reproductions of the designs are scored, and the total score is compared to the performance of other six-year-old children. This determines if the child is above average, average, or below average with respect to visual-motor development compared to other children his or her age.

Results from visual-motor testing are important because visual-motor difficulties can affect not only school achievement but other aspects of a child's life, such as riding a bike and playing ball. A visual-motor test, however, usually is used as only one part of a battery of tests rather than by itself.

Behavior Rating Scales

Another important test in the psychologist's toolbox is the behavior rating scale. Behavior rating scales are basically screening tests. Their purpose is to provide a quick snapshot of the child's behavioral functioning. They are not a substitute for a comprehensive evaluation, but they can be helpful in determining whether a more comprehensive evaluation should be pursued.

Behavior rating scales typically are completed by parents and teachers who rate the child along several behavioral dimensions. These scales are commonly used in the evaluation of children suspected of having attention-deficit/hyperactivity disorder (ADHD), but some rating scales are also designed to screen for emotional problems, such as depression, and developmental disorders, such as Asperger's disorder. Other areas measured by rating scales include oppositional behavior, inattention, perfectionism, social problems, and impulsivity.

One benefit of rating scales is that they often are designed to be completed by parents and teachers. This allows the psychologist to get a glimpse of how the child is functioning in both the home and school settings. This creates a more complete picture of the child and can be important when making certain diagnoses.

Another advantage is that some of the briefer rating scales can be completed by parents and teachers in as little as 10 to 15 minutes, and scoring can be completed in about the same amount of time. This means the time investment for busy parents, teachers, and psychologists is minimal.

Neuropsychological Testing

Neuropsychology is the study of the relationship between the brain and mental functions such as memory, attention and concentration, visual-motor coordination, perception, and language skills. A neuropsychologist is a specially trained psychologist who studies the relationship between the brain and these areas. Various standardized tests are used by the neuropsychologist, which usually consist of tests of intelligence, achievement, memory, language, and any number of other tests, depending on the problem for which the child is being referred.

Neuropsychological testing has a wide range of applications. Although it's fairly common for stroke victims, persons with head injuries, or persons with dementia to be referred for neuropsychological testing, children with suspected learning disorders, developmental delays, or attentional difficulties also are often referred.

Just like other evaluations, neuropsychological evaluations require more than just test data to form an accurate picture of the child. A thorough history, interviews, and observations are also normal parts of the evaluation process.

And because several tests may need to be administered and a large amount of information collected, the evaluation may take several hours and, therefore, may need to be completed in more than one session.

Testing Children with Disabilities

Children with disabilities, like all children, have unique strengths and weaknesses, but the nature of their disability usually presents challenges far beyond those found with children in general. When testing children with disabilities, the examiner must have the qualifications mentioned in Chapter 1, that is, the proper training and experience. Additionally, he or she should be reasonably knowledgeable about the specific disability. For example, in order to obtain valid IQ and achievement results on a child with a hearing impairment, it would be important for the psychologist or examiner to know things such as the degree of impairment, when it first began, and what communication skills the child uses. It's also important to have a basic understanding of how the impairment affects learning. This level of understanding increases the likelihood that the results will accurately represent the child.

In school settings, a *multidisciplinary team*—a group of professionals with different specialties—typically is involved when evaluating a child suspected of having a disability. A child with a speech problem, for example, may be seen by a psychologist, a speech and language pathologist, an audiologist, a dentist, a physician, and possibly others. This is to insure that all aspects of the child's disability that can affect learning are addressed.

As for the tests used to evaluate children with disabilities, they're often the same ones used to evaluate children in general, only adapted or modified. Many commonly used IQ tests, for example, require that the child work with blocks or puzzles, or look at pictures. Obviously, a child must have adequate vision in order to do these things. If these tests are used, they must be modified in order to make them appropriate for a child with a visual impairment. The changes would include omitting all tasks that require the use of vision.

For some children with visual impairments, using large-print test booklets might be just fine. For others, a tape-recorded version of the test may be required. For a child who is deaf or has a significant hearing impairment and knows sign language, having an interpreter who signs the test questions to the child will be necessary.

121

Some children with severe disabilities may not be testable with standardized tests. A psychological evaluation can still be conducted, though. The evaluation might consist of detailed interviews with parents and teachers, observations of the child at home and in the classroom, and informal assessments in academic, language, motor, and social skills.

As a parent of a child with a disability, your main concern should be whether the evaluation provides accurate and useful information. What are your child's strengths and weaknesses? What specific things can you as a parent do to help your child? What specific things can the teachers do? And most importantly, what would be the most appropriate education for your child? For parents, especially parents of a child with a disability, it's also a good idea to become familiar with certain laws.

Good IDEA

One particularly important law is the *Individuals with Disabilities Education Improvement Act of 2004* (Public Law 108-446). More commonly referred to as *IDEA 2004* (or simply *IDEA*) because it was revised and amended in 2004, this federal law guarantees a "free appropriate public education" (FAPE) to all school-age children with disabilities. The 13 disability categories included in *IDEA 2004* are:

Autism—A developmental disability that severely affects a child's ability to communicate either verbally or nonverbally, to interact with others, and to achieve in school, which is usually evident by age three.

Deaf-blindness—A simultaneous hearing and visual impairment that significantly interferes with educational performance.

Deafness—A severe hearing impairment that interferes with educational achievement.

Emotional disturbance—A condition that has one or more of the following characteristics and significantly interferes with school performance: 1) inability to learn, 2) inability to develop satisfactory relationships with peers and adults (for example, teachers), 3) having feelings and behaviors that are inappropriate to the circumstances, 4) chronic unhappiness or depressed mood, or

5) the development of physical problems or fears resulting from personal or school stresses.

Hearing impairment—Difficulty with hearing, temporary or permanent, that interferes with learning and is not included in the category of "deafness."

Mental retardation—Significantly below average intellectual functioning coexisting with significant deficits in adaptive behavior functioning/self-help skills with an onset before the age of 18 years.

Multiple disabilities—Two or more impairments, such as mental retardation and blindness, occurring simultaneously.

Orthopedic impairment—A severe orthopedic problem that interferes with a child's educational performance. Examples would include cerebral palsy, poliomyelitis, and amputations.

Other health impairment—Having limited strength, energy, and attentiveness due to a chronic or acute health problem (for example, asthma, attention-deficit/hyperactivity disorder, diabetes, heart problems) that adversely impacts a child's educational performance.

Specific learning disability—A problem with understanding or using written or spoken language that interferes with a child's ability to use language, think, listen, read, write, spell, or do math.

Speech or language impairment—This includes impairments of communication, such as stuttering, poor articulation (pronunciation of words), language impairment, or voice impairment that adversely affects school performance.

Traumatic brain injury—An injury to the brain (for example, as a result of an auto accident or other blow to the head) that results in either partial or total impairment in the ability to carry out normal day-to-day functions and interferes with educational performance.

Visual impairment (including partial sight and blindness)—Problems with vision that interfere with a child's educational performance.

The roots of *IDEA 2004* go back to 1975 when the *Education of All the Handicapped (EAH) Act* (also known as Public Law 94-142) was passed. Then, in 1986, the *EAH* was amended to include preschool children with disabilities. In 1990, additional changes were made to the *EAH* and the name was changed to *IDEA*. Further changes signed into law by President Bill Clinton in 1997 resulted in *IDEA 97*.

IDEA 97 was reauthorized by Congress and the new statute, signed into law by President George W. Bush in December 2004, is now called the *Individuals with Disabilities Education Improvement Act of 2004 (IDEA 2004)*. *IDEA 2004* includes several changes, most of which became effective in July 2005. The fundamental purpose of *IDEA* is for the millions of children with disabilities, estimated to be more than six million, to receive an appropriate education that will adequately prepare them for employment and independent living.

One change under *IDEA 2004* that relates to testing is that schools no longer are required to administer IQ and achievement tests in order to determine whether a child has a specific learning disability (SLD). Before *IDEA 2004*, schools had to show that a significant discrepancy existed between a child's intellectual ability and academic achievement levels, based on their IQ and achievement test scores. If the discrepancy was large enough, the student would be classified as learning disabled and would be eligible for special services. Although IQ and achievement tests may still be used, schools now have the option of determining whether a child has a learning disability by evaluating how that child responds to research-based educational interventions. This approach is called *response-to-intervention* (RTI).

The RTI approach has a distinct advantage over traditional IQ and achievement testing. With RTI, schools are able to quickly screen all students, beginning in kindergarten, for academic problems by using short (usually 1 to 5 minutes), easy-to-administer tests, called curriculum-based measurements. (See Chapter 4 for a more detailed discussion of curriculum-based measurement.) Students identified as having academic problems receive proven educational interventions and are frequently monitored to ensure they are making progress. If adequate progress is being made, interventions may be stopped; if not, more intense services are provided.

Does the use of RTI and curriculum-based measurements mean your child or student will not be administered a traditional IQ or achievement test, or other standardized tests? No. Even if the RTI approach determines that a child has a learning problem, traditional tests still may be used to help determine the nature of the problem.

No Child Left Behind

Another important piece of legislation signed into law by President Bush in 2002 was the *No Child Left Behind Act of 2001 (NCLB)*. *NCLB* was a reauthorization of the *Education and Secondary Education Act (ESEA)*, originally signed into law in 1965 by President Lyndon B. Johnson. *NCLB* was considered to be the most sweeping piece of educational reform legislation in modern times. The framework of *NCLB* rests on four central principles:

1. Accountability—States, school districts, and schools have the ultimate responsibility of making sure that standards are in place and that progress is being made in meeting those standards.

2. Flexibility and local control—States will have more control to determine which programs ought to receive federal education money.

3. Increased choices for parents—A parent with a child in a failing public school has the option of transferring their child to a higher achieving public school or public charter school. And federal education funds could be used to provide services such as tutoring, summer school programs, and other "supplemental educational services."

4. Proven teaching methods—A refreshing aspect of this law has to do with using sound, researched-based educational practices. As stated on the U.S. Department of Education's Web site (http://www.ed.gov/nclb/), "No Child Left Behind puts special emphasis on determining what educational programs and practices have been proven effective through rigorous scientific research."

NCLB started out as a well-intentioned piece of legislation aimed at improving public education for all children, but problems emerged at the outset. A major criticism was that *NCLB* had been grossly under-funded and, therefore, difficult to implement. Another was that it was too test-driven. This tended to encourage teaching to the test, which some feared placed too much emphasis on test scores and not enough on genuine learning. And in the 2004 book, *Many Children Left Behind*, several respected educators suggested that *NCLB* was too punitive, too reliant on norm-based tests, contributed to dropout rates, and actually hurts poor and minority children.

Perhaps the biggest criticism had to do with the goal of having all public school students proficient by 2014. This is an admirable goal, and it might be possible in a perfect world, but the world in which we live is far from perfect. Our schools are made up of diverse students, not only in terms of race and ethnicity, but in terms of their strengths and weaknesses. Some students excel at learning, while others have learning disabilities or emotional problems that make learning difficult. Some come from homes where their lives are touched by violence, poverty, drugs, or abuse, while others come from homes where money and opportunities are abundant and worries are few.

The difficulty with imposing the same standards and tests on all children, particularly those with disabilities, was highlighted by a middle school teacher in Salem, Oregon, whose comments were published in the April 2006 issue of *NEA Today* (Jehlen, 2006):

> "What if the government decided physical disabilities could be eliminated through standards? What if there were a mandate that doctors must bring their patients to 'normal standards' and all patients must be able to walk? The government does not seem to believe that our students' disabilities are real." (p. 27)

Although *NCLB* has been around since 2002, change is clearly in the air. In March 2010 President Barrack Obama proposed a major overhaul of *NCLB*, which is outlined in the U.S. Department of Education document, *A Blueprint for Reform*. This proposal includes five priorities.

1) Making sure students graduating from high school have the knowledge and skills that will make them college- or career-ready.

2) An expectation of excellence from teachers and administrators. This means having a system that identifies good teachers (based on student performance as well as other measures). Effort will be directed at rewarding and retaining good teachers and administrators and to distribute these teachers and administrators where they are needed most.

3) A system of accountability to make sure schools are adequately preparing students to meet standards for college or a career. Schools are expected to provide all students with access to a quality education, "From English Learners and students with disabilities to Native American students, homeless students, migrant students, rural students, and neglected or delinquent students" (p. 5).

4) Schools and education leaders will be expected to focus on reforms that improve student achievement. Emphasis also will be on providing a challenging high school curriculum.

5) The success of students is a shared responsibility among families, public agencies, and community organizations. New ideas that promote successful schools and successful students will be encouraged.

The final version of what *A Blueprint for Reform* will look like or how workable it will be in the everyday world of education obviously is unknown at this juncture. Testing will almost certainly continue to have an important role, but it probably will have less of a "high stakes" quality because multiple measures are likely to be used to make important decisions rather than a single test.

A Blueprint for Reform doubtfully will be able to shake off all the negative publicity of standardized testing that was spawned by *NCLB's* high-stakes philosophy, and a fresh start does appear to be badly needed. Testing perhaps never deserved the revered status it was given by educational policymakers, politicians, and even parents and teachers to a degree. *A Blueprint for Reform* could mark the beginning of a new era for educational testing...one that recognizes that a student is much more than a test score.

CHAPTER 8

Helping Children Do Their Best

The world is filled with individuals who have faced significant challenges, many of whom have achieved great success in life. They include artists, scientists, politicians, athletes, writers, explorers, and business leaders. This is a testament to the adaptability of human beings and to the strength of the human spirit.

S o many things can interfere with test performance. When we think of all the obstacles that a fairly large number of children have to contend with on a daily basis, it's amazing that these children do as well as they do. Although these obstacles can make learning and life more difficult, in almost all instances something can be done to lessen their effects.

Obstacles to Performance

Some common obstacles that can hinder a child's test performance include test anxiety, a disability (learning, physical, or emotional), lack of opportunities, and what a child believes about him or herself. How much these will impact a child's test performance depends, of course, on the child's inner resources, support systems, and unique set of circumstances. We'll start off with a quick look at each of these obstacles and then touch on some general ideas that might be helpful to parents.

Test Anxiety

Do children really become nervous when taking tests, or are we exaggerating the matter of test anxiety? A 2002 survey sponsored by Public Agenda, a non-profit research organization, and *Education Week*, a weekly educational newspaper, showed that "only five percent" of a national sample of 600 middle school and high school students said they become so anxious that they are unable to take proficiency tests. This is compared to 73 percent who said they get nervous but are still able to manage taking the test, and 23 percent who reported not becoming nervous at all.

Five percent does seem like a small number, but if we apply that to all students in the United States, it swells to two and a half million students. And that figure represents only the extreme group—those who are unable to take the test because of high anxiety. A large number—73 percent—said they become nervous but are still able to handle the test. If that percentage is applied nationwide, that's a staggering 37 million students. And although these students are able to get through the test, their anxiety could still be lowering their test performance.

To professionals experienced with treating anxiety disorders, test anxiety is real. It's when a child becomes extremely nervous and tense, usually immediately before and during the test. In severe cases, the child may literally tremble with fear in anticipation of taking a test, sometimes even becoming ill and throwing up. If we could peer into the mind of the child while taking the test, we would see a lot of self-doubt and negative thinking. After the test, you may hear comments like, "My mind went blank," or "I was so nervous that I forgot everything I studied."

Some children are more prone to test anxiety than others. For example, children with learning disabilities seem to suffer more test anxiety than children without learning disabilities (Sena, Lowe, & Lee, 2007). But test anxiety can touch anyone. The common thread is that children with test anxiety all suffer from terrible pangs of nervousness in test situations and in situations where they are judged or have to perform, often because of a fear of failure.

If a child's level of anxiety is severe and regularly causes distress or interferes with school performance, professional help may be needed. But not all anxiety is bad. The extremes of anxiety—a lot of anxiety (worries way too much) or no anxiety at all (could care less)—are usually what interferes with test performance. A little bit of anxiety, though, can be helpful because it serves to motivate the child to study and to do well.

Learning Disability

Estimates of the number of individuals with specific learning disabilities vary considerably. According to the U.S. Department of Education, the number of public school children in 2006-07 with learning disabilities being served by federal programs was about five and one-half percent. Like individuals with other disabilities, a person with a learning disability certainly is not doomed to a life of failure. Most, in fact, will lead successful and productive lives. In order to be successful and productive, however, it's important for a child with a learning disability to receive education that is tailored to his or her specific strengths and needs and to start this education as early as possible.

A child with a learning disability has a genuine problem with learning. He or she studies, puts forth an earnest effort to do well, but still has trouble learning. Often it's in a particular subject area, such as reading, arithmetic, writing, or understanding language, but it could be in more than one area.

A child with a learning disability is not lazy, is not being intentionally difficult, and is not "dumb." Punishing or demeaning the child in an attempt to "straighten 'em out" won't help and will only cause him or her to be more frustrated. Better results are obtained with support and encouragement, by knowing your child's strengths and weaknesses, and by making sure your child is getting the right kind of educational instruction as early as possible.

Physical Disability

According to U.S. Department of Education data for 2006-07, the percentage of children between the ages of 3 and 21 with physical disabilities (e.g., orthopedic impairments, visual impairments, multiple disabilities, other health impairments, traumatic brain injury) receiving services from federally supported school programs was just shy of two percent. Children with physical disabilities are faced with many of the same, and sometimes more, of the problems and frustrations as children with other types of disabilities. A paraplegic child will have to take tests designed specifically for him or her rather than standard paper-and-pencil tests. A child with a hearing impairment may have to take the test with the aid of an interpreter. A child with blindness may have to take a Braille or tape-recorded version of the test and have someone record the responses on paper. Regardless of the disability, accommodations must be made so that the test will measure the child's knowledge accurately.

Emotional Disability

U.S. Department of Education data indicate that for 2006-07 approximately one percent of children between the ages of 3 and 21 were being served in federally supported school programs because of an "emotional disturbance." This figure almost certainly is lower than the number of school-age children actually experiencing emotional problems because not all children with emotional problems will meet the federal definition.

Earlier estimates indicate that as many as 220 out of 1000 students (or 22 percent) in a typical school could have a diagnosable psychiatric disorder (Doll, 1996). And Leaf et al. (1996) noted that nearly 21 percent of children ages 9 to 17 have a diagnosable mental disorder or substance abuse problem sufficient enough to cause minimal impairment. This number drops to 11 percent when taking into account only those who are significantly impaired, and to 5 percent for those who are extremely impaired. Considering that even the smallest of these estimates represents millions of children, one quickly gets a sense of the impact that emotional problems can have on the lives of children.

Children with emotional problems tend to do poorer on tests and with their schoolwork than children in general. The more severe the emotional problem, the poorer the child likely will do on intelligence and achievement tests. For some children, their problems may be short-lived or not particularly severe, and the negative effect on tests or school performance may be minimal and temporary. For others, the problems may persist to the point where professional treatment is necessary. It is important not to ignore serious emotional problems in hopes that the child will "grow out of it." For most children, that doesn't happen.

Lack of Opportunity

Some children simply have not had adequate educational or learning opportunities to do well in school and, as a result, they do not do well in their schoolwork and on tests. The reasons for this are many—poverty, chaotic home environment, abuse and neglect, or a climate of discouragement.

It's expected that schools will provide its students with an array of educational opportunities. Outside of school, though, parents must assume the primary responsibility of providing opportunities for their child. This may be difficult for some because of financial circumstances, but many valuable things don't have a high price tag. It may be an occasional word of hope or encouragement, a smile of approval, or a warm and loving hug. It may be buying a new book and reading it together, taking a walk in the park, visiting a museum or library, helping with homework, laughing together over a silly story, or simply taking a walk together and talking about "things."

In different ways, each of these activities provides important opportunities—the opportunity to develop hope, to develop self-acceptance, to develop meaningful relationships, and to learn by reading, sharing experiences, observation, and discussion. And they also convey to your child something that is especially important—that you care.

What Your Child Believes About Him or Herself

The choices we make on a day-to-day basis are largely determined by our belief systems. We vote for a particular political candidate based on our political beliefs. We belong to a particular religious denomination (or choose not to belong) based on our religious beliefs. We choose friends based on whether we believe them to be honest, dependable, and likable. Our biases and prejudices are based on strongly held beliefs about particular groups of people, religion, politics, or any number of things. And our moral actions are based on what we believe to be right and wrong.

Our belief system includes self-beliefs, which can be extremely powerful influences in a person's life. If these beliefs are mostly positive, they can open up gateways to success; if mostly negative, they can be roadblocks in life.

Imagine identical twins, a brother and sister, with the same IQ. Let's say that the brother believes a lot of negative things about himself, like "I'm dumb," "I can't do anything right," and "No one cares," because for most of his life he had been told over and over what he had done wrong and rarely what he had done right. And let's say that his sister, in contrast, believes a lot of positive things about herself, like, "I'm a hard worker," "I never give up," and "I'm a good student," because she usually had been told what she had done right. Which of these two children do you think is likely to do better in school? If you guessed the sister, you would be right.

133

It is far more important to let your children know when they do things well than when they mess up. And, of course, they will mess up from time to time because, as human beings, we are not perfect. But that's OK because making mistakes and failing are needed for learning to take place. A good rule of thumb is to find something positive to say about your child—and be sincere about it—at least once a day. Focusing on the genuinely positive aspects of a child's life rather than the negatives can help foster a positive self-image and increase self-confidence.

Ways to Help Your Child

Imagine that it's one week before the proficiency test. The excitement at school is more apparent than in previous weeks. In many school districts, this week is filled with activities similar to those that often are seen the week before a championship football game in high school. For the championship game, the principal delivers an uplifting message during morning announcements. Bright banners beaming with school colors are plastered across hallways. Cheerleaders get the crowd chanting familiar slogans during the traditional all-school pep rally, climaxed by inspiring words from the coach.

All this attention is aimed at raising the spirits and self-confidence of students—especially those on the team. The message? If we think we are winners, then we are winners. And it's a good message to deliver in any situation. It promotes a positive attitude. When it comes to proficiency tests, the same "championship" concept is used in many school districts. After all, much is riding on these tests.

Schools usually do the lion's share of "pre-game" activities when it comes to preparing for proficiency tests. Teachers in general do reviews in the classroom and give practice tests to familiarize students with the procedures. The teachers also may talk about things such as the importance of reading directions carefully, what steps to take when stymied by a question, watching the clock to pace oneself and to finish as much of the test as possible, knowing whether to answer the easy or difficult questions first, or deciding what to do if none of the answers seem to be correct.

To raise spirits, principals, who often are busy with duties in the front office, suddenly find themselves entering classrooms to talk with students about pride and trying their best. And teachers have been known to promise the children an afternoon of fun—treats and games—if they show up for school during proficiency week and do their very best.

One school district in the Midwest had small groups of students meet with the school psychologist to discuss how to overcome butterflies in the stomach, general nervousness, and fear of the test. The discussion touched on subjects such as relaxation breathing techniques and phrases students could say to themselves to lift their spirits, reduce fear, and heighten motivation.

By the time the week of the proficiency test rolls around, parents can do little to help their child study for the test. At this late stage, the student either knows the material or not. Still, at the very least, parents should calmly talk to their child about why the test is important and encourage them to try their best.

What follows are several tips that can be used to help a child to prepare for tests. They can be used for classroom tests, proficiency tests, college admission tests, or any test or performance situation. And, as you will see, most are easy to implement.

Studying

This means studying days before the test and not waiting until the last minute. Adequate preparation reduces stress and anxiety and leads to better classroom test scores and grades. Many parents complain that their children don't know how to study effectively. Here are some simple ways to improve studying.

- *Be systematic.* Start from the beginning and read everything (including the directions) through to the end. Don't skip anything.

- *Break up study time into short periods.* These study periods can range from around 15 to 45 minutes, depending on the age of the child, with shorter periods for younger children or those with short attention spans. It is far more effective to study this way than to study for hours at a time without any breaks.

- *Offer help if needed.* It's more effective and more efficient for a parent to take five minutes to teach a difficult concept than to have their child stumble along and waste 30 minutes of valuable time with trial-and-error learning.

- *Review what has been studied.* It can be especially helpful if parents help their child review the material when done studying. This strengthens what the child has learned.

Studying does not have to be excessive in order to be effective. For example, 15 minutes of effective studying will be better than 30 minutes of unfocused studying. *And the sooner your child learns effective study habits, the better.* Effective studying can have a significant effect on classroom tests. If your child learns effective study habits early in life, this likely will help to improve their performance on classroom work, on classroom tests, and on the standardized tests that they will encounter later in their education.

If your teenage daughter or son is preparing for a standardized test such as the SAT, taking sample tests under the exact conditions (e.g., the same amount of time and the same time of day) as the actual SAT may help. As mentioned earlier, sample tests can be found in study guides available at most bookstores, and relatively inexpensive computer software programs for college admissions tests are readily available as well. Obviously, the questions on these sample tests will not be the actual test questions, but they will be similar. In fact, some of the questions may have been used on previous versions of the test. Taking these practice tests is always a good idea. Doing so will give your son or daughter a feel for the format of the test and a feel for what it's like working under timed conditions.

Aside from increasing learning and improving grades, another important but less obvious advantage of studying is that it increases self-esteem. Ask a child how they feel when they do well on a test and you'll almost always hear that they feel good. The reason is that doing well gives a child a sense of *competence*, which is the foundation for building self-confidence.

This is not only true for school subjects but for all performance areas of life (and by the way, it's true for adults as well). For example, a child who practices (which is a form of studying) long hours in order to become a better basketball player will almost certainly become a better player…and a more confident one. In other words, hard work pays off, whether in school or in life.

Get a good night's rest and eat well

Parents should make sure their child gets a good night's sleep before any test. This could have as much of an impact on a child's test performance as the psychological and spirit-raising activities. A well-rested child is a child ready to concentrate and work. It is difficult to do well on a test, and in many other things in life for that matter, if your child does not get a good night's rest. Adequate sleep improves concentration and attention, and as an added benefit, your child also is likely to be less cranky and irritable.

Eating a nutritious breakfast and lunch will help, too. Some children do go to school hungry, and for them their focus is on their grumbling stomach rather than schoolwork. That's just one reason why school breakfast and lunch programs are so important.

Dress comfortably

Make sure your child is dressed in something that is physically and emotionally comfortable. If a child hates the shirt he's wearing and feels self-conscious, he may waste time worrying about what other kids think rather than focusing on the test. The same goes if the pants are too tight or the dress too short. Pulling and tugging on ill-fitting clothes takes time away from concentrating on the test questions

Breathe properly and relax

If your child is prone to test anxiety or anxiety in general, it may be a good idea to have him or her learn some simple breathing and relaxation techniques. These are techniques that can be learned quickly and used in most anxiety-producing situations your child will encounter, such as taking a test or giving a talk in class. Excellent resources are the school counselor and school psychologist. For children who suffer from severe anxiety, more intensive professional help may be needed. It should be fairly easy to find a mental health professional in the community who is skilled at teaching relaxation techniques because anxiety is such a common problem. The good news is this—anxiety is very treatable.

Use appropriate self-talk strategies

Teach your child to use positive and rational self-talk. For example, "I will do my best," or "The world won't end if I don't do well," or "I will concentrate and stay focused," or "I will read the instructions carefully before I begin." These are much better than self-talk that increases anxiety, such as, "I know I'm going to fail," "I don't know what I'm doing," "Everyone is smarter than I am," "I'm just stupid," or "I can't do this." Positive and rational self-talk, of course, isn't enough—your child must also be prepared, by studying. Again, excellent resources to help your child learn positive and rational self-talk are the school counselor and psychologist.

Do fun enrichment activities

It's important for parents to talk, read, and interact with their children. Play board games and memory games, encourage him or her to watch educational TV programs, take nature walks, measure the dimensions of your house, discuss news events, and visit museums, parks, and zoos. At dinner, ask your child his or her opinion about things and listen, even if you happen to disagree with what they have to say. This shows your child that you consider his or her views to be important, which conveys respect. and it also can help to increase self-confidence.

Be positive and offer encouragement

Many parents are quick to point out what their child got wrong on a homework assignment or test. A far better approach is to point out what he or she got right, even if it is one itsy bitsy question. Then encourage your child by telling him or her that they will be learning more and that they will be doing better (with your help). Help your child to achieve success by being available to review homework or to offer assistance. If you do not have the time or the expertise in certain subjects, you may want to consider hiring a good tutor. Tutoring is a form of personalized instruction and can be very helpful. And, of course, praise your child for successes and any genuine effort he or she puts forth.

Make learning meaningful

If you want to help your young child learn basic math skills, such as addition, you could simply encourage the rote memorization of addition facts. This will help, but by adding something meaningful to this age-old strategy, you can make learning even more effective. For example, you and your child could count the number of trees in the back yard and add this to the number of trees in the front yard, or count the number of dresses in your daughter's closet and add them to the number of dresses in your closet. Research has shown that children (and adults) learn more effectively if what they are learning has some practical meaning.

Encourage thinking and reasoning skills

Discuss with your child things such as how birds fly, how we know wind exists, why the concept of time is important, or any other type of "thinking" question. Be prepared to offer clear explanations, and together look up the answers to questions you can't answer.

Looking at how things are similar (analogies) also can be a helpful way to foster reasoning skills. For example, you might discuss how a book and a letter are alike (they both use words to express ideas), how a bird and a plant are alike (they're both living things), or in what way a lake and a desert are the same (they're both part of nature).

Some experts believe that children who are taught these types of analytical and abstract reasoning skills do better on standardized tests than those who aren't. Although the evidence on this is not conclusive, there are strong indications that encouraging your child to reason analytically and abstractly can be beneficial in general.

Be informed

Know your child's teacher, know what is being taught in the classroom and, if you have a child with a disability, know the laws that affect your child, like the *Individuals with Disabilities Education Improvement Act of 2004 (IDEA 2004)* and *No Child Left Behind (NCLB)*. Any educational planning for a child, such as developing an Individual Education Plan (IEP) for children receiving special education instruction, should involve the parents. In this modern age, it's common to find households where either both parents work or the household is headed by a single parent. Understandably, you may not have the time to visit your child's teacher or attend meetings. If not, call your child's teacher at a convenient time to request information, offer suggestions, ask questions, and express any concerns.

Another way to keep informed is to join a parent support group. Many of these groups meet after work for the convenience of working parents. You might be surprised at how much can be learned at these meetings. Many parents have become experts on disabilities and laws affecting children with disabilities and on other school issues because of their active involvement with these types of groups. Moreover, parent groups have become extremely powerful forces over the years and have been able to bring about significant changes in laws. And if you have access to a computer (if not, most public libraries offer computer services), the Internet is bulging with information on just about any subject on education you can imagine, and much of it is specifically designed for parents.

Start your own support group

"There's power in numbers" is a truism that's hard to ignore. Speak with parents at Parent Teacher Organization (PTO) meetings and with friends and neighbors to find out who might be interested in participating in a parent discussion group on school testing practices. You might find at first that parents are not interested or don't want to rock the boat, but as word gets around, the idea may catch on. As other parents find that they share your concerns, they may be more willing to attend. One of the wonderful things about groups such as these is that parents immediately learn that they are not alone in their concerns.

The key to sparking the interest of parents, who seem to be busier and busier with each passing day, is to make the meeting worth their while. Promote it as a meeting in which they will be making an investment in their child. You can do this by scheduling special speakers. Start with a school principal who may have some insight into how tests are recorded on the permanent record or how they are being used to place children in certain classes such as remedial reading. Follow up with a school counselor who can inform parents about their legal rights in regards to seeing their children's test scores and other items in the permanent record. Experts on how to prepare a child for taking a test and how to help a child learn better in school also may be helpful. You may also want to invite a local psychologist who is a test expert to discuss the pros and cons of testing.

Although the topics covered in these groups will be limited only by your imagination, it is a good idea to keep a specific purpose in mind, such as to discuss school testing practices; otherwise, they very easily could evolve into watered-down meetings where everything from cafeteria food to dress code to bus scheduling is discussed. The group also should operate from a spirit of cooperation with schools. The objective is not to antagonize school officials but to learn from them (and for them to learn from you) and to work with them in the best interest of children. After all, everyone should have the same goal—to help each and every child learn and perform at his or her best.

Use individualized instruction and interventions that work

Individualized instruction means teaching to a child's specific strengths and remediating weaknesses. It is not a general approach you would find in a typical classroom setting where the teacher has the daunting task of teaching 25 or more children at the same time, all with different ability levels, different personalities, and different motivational levels. Individualized instruction is specific; it is geared to the individual child. Tutoring is an example of individualized instruction because it focuses on a single child's educational needs, not the needs of a group of children. The tutoring, though, must be based on specific strategies or interventions that have been proven to be effective. We're in the era of data-driven education where educators must now prove that what they do really works. In simple terms, the student must make progress.

For parents with a child who receives special education instruction, you probably will be familiar with a plan that emphasizes individualized instruction called the Individual Educational Plan (IEP). Your child's IEP is designed specifically for him or her—no one else. Why individualized instruction? Because it's more effective than group instruction for children having problems with learning.

Understand the importance of school attendance

The instruction a child receives in school will be the main source of knowledge and skills that ultimately will make him or her successful in life. And in order for a child to acquire this knowledge and these skills, he or she must be in school on a consistent basis. There may be times when the student will miss a day or two because of an illness or to observe a religious holiday, but those absences should be infrequent over the course of their education.

For children who are home schooled, they too must attend their "home school" regularly in order for effective learning to occur. In situations where a child cannot attend school because of a serious illness or disability, some form of alternative education, such as homebound instruction, must be provided on a consistent basis. Overall, despite the criticisms of schools seen in newspaper headlines across the country and on TV news programs lamenting "schools in crisis," or "the ills of education," teachers do a good job of educating our children. But a child must be in school in order to reap the benefits.

Seek professional assistance when needed

If a child is suffering from an emotional or behavioral problem that is interfering with schoolwork or with normal day-to-day affairs, it may be necessary to consider help from a qualified professional. This could be a psychologist, psychiatrist, counselor, or social worker. Ignoring a problem and hoping it will go away could make it worse.

The problem may be something minor that has a simple solution. In this case, whatever burden was on the child's shoulders could be quickly lifted and he or she can move on. Other situations may be more serious and require longer treatment or therapy. In either case, the sooner proper help is sought, the faster the child will find relief and do better in school and on tests.

Let your child be a child

Some parents have become so obsessed with having their children become successful in school and ultimately in life that they place excessive learning demands on their children beginning in infancy. A *Time* magazine story reported that too much early academic stimulation may not be as beneficial as was once thought (Kluger & Park, 2001). Instead, children may benefit more from learning one of the most fundamental sets of skills—social skills. That is, learning how to get along with others—whether it is taking turns on the swing at the playground, sharing toys, talking with a friend about a trip to the zoo, or playing dolls with a friend.

Providing a child with different social experiences and guiding him or her to learn the skills that lead to successful social relations often allow a child to flourish both socially and academically, more than rigidly programming a child from a very early age with intense academic stimulation. Research reported in *Monitor on Psychology* indicates that students who participate in formal social and emotional learning (SEL) programs tend to show better achievement-test performance, improved mental health, and an increase in social competence (DeAngelis, 2010). As a parent, the important thing is to find a healthy balance between helping your child develop social-emotional competence and providing him or her with developmentally appropriate amounts of academic stimulation.

Reduce stress

Do children experience stress? It's easy to think of children as being carefree and not having a worry in the world. After all, they don't have to be concerned about the monthly mortgage payment or other bills that need to be paid on a regular basis. They don't have to worry about making appointments, taking the family car in for repairs, filing taxes, or calling a repair person when the furnace stops working on a cold winter's night. But, like adults, children do face stress in their lives.

Stress is a part of everyone's life, including children. Sometimes the stress is short-lived and passes quickly. Other times it's chronic and seems to hang on forever. It's impossible to eliminate stress completely, but learning effective coping strategies can reduce its ill effects.

The symptoms shown by a child under stress vary. The child may internalize the stress (turn it inward) and develop physical symptoms such as headaches, stomachaches, or other aches and pains that have no physical explanation. The child may also show other types of symptoms such as difficulty falling asleep, excessive worrying, or fearful behavior. Some children may externalize the stress (turn it outward) and engage in acting-out behavior such as fighting, or being verbally aggressive.

Children experience stress in any number of ways. It may be a boy being threatened by the class bully, a girl sitting in class wondering if her parents are going to get a divorce, a girl not knowing how to explain a failing grade to her parents, or a boy being upset because no one wants to play with him during recess. Other examples of stress include being a victim of abuse or neglect, being exposed to violence in the home or neighborhood, having surgery, dealing with a serious illness, death of a family member, breaking up with a boyfriend/girlfriend, transferring to a new school, or moving to a new city.

Whatever the source, helping children to cope effectively with stress is important. Minor day-to-day stresses often can be dealt with fairly easily and effectively. Here are some tips for parents:

- Provide a safe, secure, and relatively predictable home environment.

- Let your child know you care for and love her or him.

- Focus on solutions, and discuss appropriate solutions to problems.

- Select appropriate television programs rather than those that produce fears and anxieties.

- Encourage your child to talk about his or her fears and worries, and genuinely listen.

- Acknowledge those times when he or she deals successfully with stress.

- Teach (by example) effective ways to get through those "bumps in the road."

- Encourage choices, and be supportive of your child's decisions.

- Discuss with your child expected changes (for example, moving to a new neighborhood).

- Encourage support systems such as friendships, or belonging to a group or club.

- Teach your child that making mistakes is part of life and that we learn from our mistakes.

- Keep lines of communication open; be available to talk to your child.

- Help your child to be organized, to get homework done and turned in on time, and to be prepared for exams.

Prolonged or severe stress not only can affect a child's performance in school but also his or her overall physical and psychological well-being. Helping the child who is experiencing chronic or severe stress often is beyond the ability and personal resources of a parent. In these situations, professional guidance should be sought. Again, good starting points are the school counselor and the school psychologist; the child's pediatrician or a qualified mental health professional within the community are other resources to consider.

Be involved

One of the simplest yet most important ways for a parent to help their child do better in school is to be involved in their child's education. This may include attending PTA meetings or open house activities at your child's school, communicating regularly with your child's teacher, and attending parent-teacher conferences.

Reading with your child, helping with homework, and simply having a positive attitude toward education also are important. Rather than simply saying that you care, doing these types of activities show that you care, and they increase the likelihood that your son or daughter will adopt that part of your value system that says education is important.

Many parents encounter common obstacles that prevent them from following through with many of these seemingly simple things. If both parents work, for example, free time is likely to be at a premium. In single-parent households, especially those with more than one child, time may be even more precious. And in single-parent homes where the parent also is employed, juggling even the smallest of responsibilities can be exceedingly difficult.

Less obvious obstacles also may keep a parent from becoming involved in their child's education. Embarrassment over poor English-speaking skills, shyness, feeling intimidated by school personnel, or a personal dislike of school may keep some parents from visiting the school. And a parent with a serious emotional disorder or an addiction problem may find it next to impossible to become involved with school activities.

If a parent cannot make it to school for whatever reason, the situation is not hopeless. Something can still be done. Most importantly, they should try to schedule time with their child at home, much in the way they would schedule an appointment. During this time, reading to your child, helping with homework, or discussing current events may be all that you can offer for the time being, but it is something, and it is important.

CHAPTER 9

Frequently Asked Questions
About Testing

This chapter provides a glimpse of the concerns that many parents have expressed about testing. These are actual questions, and as you look over them, you may come to realize that you are not alone in terms of how you feel about tests. If you have a question relating to your child's particular circumstance, it is recommended that you consult with a professional experienced with educational and psychological testing.

*****

I'm curious about my daughter's IQ. Should I have her tested?

Unless your child is having problems, or you suspect she is gifted or talented, she probably doesn't need to be tested. Curiosity generally is not a good reason to have a child tested.

Who can I ask to have my child tested?

If you feel that your child needs to be tested/evaluated, the place to start is with the teacher. Arrange to meet with your child's teacher to discuss why you feel testing is necessary and how it may be helpful. The teacher will discuss the situation with the principal who often will be the one who makes the actual referral for testing.

If you do not wish to go through the school system, you can choose to have a qualified psychologists affiliated with a local community mental health clinic or with private practices in your community do the testing. The school district is required by law to consider the results from this "independent evaluation"; however, the school district is not required to accept the findings or recommendations.

Can I get a second opinion if I don't agree with the school's testing results?

The short answer is yes. School districts have a procedure for obtaining a second opinion called an Independent Educational Evaluation (IEE). You should be aware that the results of the second evaluation may not be significantly different from those of the initial testing. If the retesting is shortly after the initial testing (for example, a month), the retesting results may be slightly higher due to a "practice effect," but they still may not be significantly different. But if you feel that the first testing simply does not reflect your child's abilities or skills accurately, it certainly is appropriate to ask for a second opinion, especially if the results are to be used to make important educational decisions.

How much will the testing cost?

If your child's teacher, and ultimately the principal, makes the referral for testing and the testing is approved, you will incur no cost. That's because the testing usually will be conducted by a school psychologist and other professionals employed or contracted by the school system. If parents wish to pursue an independent second opinion, like the Independent Educational Evaluation (IEE) mentioned above, the parents generally will be responsible for the cost; however, there are exceptions. For detailed information on this and other *IDEA* issues, an excellent resource that will inform you of procedural guidelines and your rights is the U.S. Department of Education's Web site at http:// idea.ed.gov/. Another usually excellent resource is your state's department of education Web site.

The cost of an independent evaluation from a private psychologist can vary greatly, depending on the number and types of tests administered, the time it takes to gather information from parents and teachers, and the time it takes to interpret the results and write the report. The cost could be several hundred dollars to a couple thousand dollars or even more, depending on how extensive the evaluation is. It's always a good idea to ask beforehand what the actual cost of the evaluation will be. Do not rely on your insurance to pay; insurance companies often do not cover this type of service.

My son scored very high on an IQ test. Should I ask to have him advanced a grade in school?

Advancing a grade in school may be appropriate for some children, but results from a single test should not be the only deciding factor. Other important considerations include whether the child has done well in the past, teachers' recommendations, and whether he is emotionally ready for such a change. For example, does he get along well with children, will he be socially isolated or fit in with older students, or does he even want to be advanced?

Unlike years ago, most school districts today have special programs, such as gifted or enrichment programs, for children who excel in school. Placement in one of these programs may be preferred to advancing a child a grade because it allows the child to learn from important peer-group experiences and at the same time receive more challenging instruction. Overall, it is important for gifted children to receive some type of enriched or accelerated instruction in order to nurture their abilities or talents.

My son didn't do well on his school proficiency test. Should I consider having him held back?

To hold a child back in grade is one of the most important and among the most agonizing decisions a parent can make. Common worries include, "His classmates will make fun of him," "She'll be behind all her friends," "He'll be bigger than his classmates," "He'll see himself as a failure for the rest of his life," or "Her self-esteem will be affected." These are all legitimate concerns. Although it's common for parents to be plagued with uncertainty or to feel pressured by school personnel to retain a child, this is a decision that should not be rushed.

In order to make the best decision possible, it's important to obtain as much information as possible about your child. *The decision to retain a child should never be based on test scores alone.* Doing so assumes that test scores are perfect, which they are not. Past and present test scores, past and present classroom performance, classroom observation, teacher recommendations, and what you know about your child all should be considered when such an important and potentially life-changing decision is to be made.

149

A growing body of evidence suggests that holding a child back in grade may be more harmful than beneficial. Some experts consider retention to be nothing more than a rehashing of the same material the child is already known to have difficulty with and believe that it contributes to higher dropout rates. Besides that, other potential problems include an increase in behavior problems, poor long-term gains in achievement, and difficulty with social relationships. Still, some see it as appropriate because it allows time for the child to mature and to learn the material. In reality, though, in those rare instances when a child should be retained, a concerted educational effort should be directed toward building on strengths and remediating weaknesses rather exposing the child to the same frustrations for another year.

Can test scores change?

Yes, especially if the child was not motivated to do well on the test and was just "going through the motions," or maybe he or she was ill, or simply was having a bad day. In general, however, IQ scores are fairly stable over time and are not expected to change by much. If a child is retested using the same or similar IQ test, it is expected that their retest score will be close to the score on the first test. Achievement tests are a bit different. Because achievement tests measure what a child has learned in specific academic areas, scores on these tests often can be improved by studying. This is particularly true of classroom tests. In fact, studying is one of the most effective ways to improve classroom test scores and grades.

My daughter just missed getting into the gifted program by a few points. I know she's very bright, and she easily gets bored in class. Is there anything I can do to help her?

Many things can be done. Because a child does not formally get into a gifted or enrichment program or similar program your school may offer, life does not stop, and your child's learning does not stop. So, absolutely do not give up. Many parents rely too much on schools to provide their children with exciting and challenging materials. If your child is bright (or if he or she is average, below average, or wherever), do things with him or her. Visit the zoo or the museum. Take a field trip to a local park or in your own backyard and discuss the various types of trees and plant life. Encourage reading by buying books on subjects your child is interested in. Buy fun math and reading books that can be found at most bookstores. Teach your child how to make a meal, the proper way to set a table, or how to change the oil filter on the family car. These are all forms of learning.

You also might want to find out what the gifted classes in your school actually do and try to do those activities with your child. Just because your school is not doing these extra things for your child doesn't mean you can't. Parents, regardless of their own educational level, can be highly effective teachers for their children, but they must be willing to assume this role. Children have a natural curiosity about so many things in life that parents can foster. And remember to be positive about learning.

Who makes up the achievement and proficiency tests that my child has to take in school?

A team of experts creates standardized achievement and proficiency tests. This team may consist of psychologists, educators, researchers, statisticians, and possibly others who work with a publishing company. In some cases, parents may be involved with reviewing or developing test questions.

Despite the criticisms of these tests, they generally are designed to meet high technical standards. Of course, they are not perfect. No test is. But a test doesn't have to be perfect in order to be useful, but it must meet certain technical specifications. Often, it is not the publishing company but the users of tests, such as schools, colleges and universities, and large and small companies that place too much emphasis on tests. In fact, most publishing companies will state openly that test scores should not be the only factor in making a decision about an individual.

I've been told that my child is an underachiever. What does that mean? What can I, as a parent, do?

Underachievement is a term generally used by educators to describe a child who is learning less than he or she is capable of learning. For example, a teacher may consider a particular child to be bright, but this child may be doing average work in the classroom and receiving mostly "C's" on classroom tests. Other phrases teachers may use to describe an "underachiever" are "She's not working up to her potential," "I know he can do better," or "He's not applying himself."

The reasons for underachievement are varied. Disinterest in schoolwork seems to be the cardinal reason, but other factors also may come into play. Difficulty with attention and concentration, learning disabilities, vision and hearing problems, poverty, emotional problems, or a combination of these are among the many other possible reasons for underachievement.

Trying to motivate an underachieving child can be a frustrating experience for parents. Some things parents can do to help include: making sure your child is using effective study habits, letting your child know that you are interested in how they are doing in school (e.g., by talking about their day in school and attending teacher's conferences), identifying areas where he or she is having difficulty and working on strengthening those areas, being supportive, and of course, making learning fun and interesting.

Don't tests really measure speed rather than knowledge?

The idea that tests are more a measure of speed than actual knowledge has some merit and applies mainly to proficiency tests and IQ tests because these types of tests usually have timed components. With these tests, the child must complete the test, or certain elements of the test, within a specified period of time. Other tests, such as personality tests, generally are not timed.

To illustrate how time can affect test scores, consider this real-life example: The parents of a fourth-grade girl vented their frustrations during a parent-teacher conference because their daughter was doing well in math overall (she had a B+ average) but consistently was receiving Ds or Fs on timed classroom tests. What was so frustrating to the parents was that their daughter had little difficulty with untimed classroom math tests, even though the problems on these tests (e.g., $4326 + 2671 + 348 = _____$) were considerably more difficult than problems on the timed test (e.g., $8 + 7 = \_\_\_$, $6 + 4 = \_\_\_$). Obviously, it wasn't that their daughter didn't know how to do the easier problems; she simply didn't work fast enough to complete the problems within the allowed period of time. So, to some degree, timed tests do measure how quickly a child can complete the test rather than the child's actual knowledge of the subject.

My son's IQ was 105 the first time he was tested and 116 the second time. Why the difference? Did he get smarter?

Chances are he was smarter to begin with. The difference in IQ scores could be due to a number of things. It could be because of different tests being used, or it could be due to your son being more rested, more motivated, or having less things on his mind during the second testing. If the same tests were used and the time lapse between the two tests was more than a year, the higher score is generally considered to be the more accurate score because a person cannot "fake good" on an intelligence test. In other words, you can't know more than you know. (The reverse, though, is not true; a person can "fake bad.")

My eighth-grade daughter did not get into an advanced language arts/ reading class because her score on the reading portion of the proficiency test was just two points short of the required score. Should I fight to get her in or just leave it alone?

Ideally, test scores should not be interpreted in isolation, but as parents, we know they often are. The goal is to make sure your daughter is sufficiently challenged but not to the point where she gets in over her head and begins to get discouraged and lose interest in reading. In order to make the decision "to fight or not to fight," it's important to look beyond the score. How has she done in the past? Has she *consistently* been a good reader? Have her past test scores been *consistently* high or *consistently* close to the cutoff score? Has she *consistently* received good grades in language arts and reading? Does she love to read or maybe has a passion for writing poems or stories?

Fighting with facts will be far more effective than fighting with emotion, so be sure to arm yourself with hard facts about your child's performance. If the facts show that your daughter has a history of high achievement in language arts and reading, then a meeting with your child's teacher or principal certainly would be appropriate. Of course, there's no guarantee that the decision will be changed even when all the facts are presented, but the chances will be far better.

My son was tested in school and when we had a meeting to go over the results, I had no idea what everyone was talking about. Why do test scores and the special names they use have to be so confusing?

It certainly is true that schools speak in a special language of letters (FAPE, IDEA, MFE, IEP, SLD, ADA, ED, PTA, DOE, OT, PT) and numbers (think of all the different types of scores found in a student's proficiency test report or in a Multifactored Evaluation, which is what schools refer to as an MFE). Those letters or acronyms usually pose little problem because all you have to do is ask the school psychologist, teacher, or principal what they mean. FAPE, for example, stands for <u>F</u>ree <u>A</u>ppropriate <u>P</u>ublic <u>E</u>ducation. Scores on test reports, however, are more complicated, and parents often complain they don't understand what they really mean. For some parents the scores are either too complicated or are not explained clearly. Or the report simply lacks enough information about their child's performance, and the parents are left with a narrow understanding of how their child is doing. Oftentimes, parents end up more confused than informed.

The goal of these testing reports should be to make the results clear and informative. If you have questions about your child's testing results and don't understand the scores fully, make arrangements to meet with the teacher, counselor, psychologist, or principal. Make sure the explanations you get are in terms you understand and are not loaded with technical jargon. Test scores, no matter how complicated they seem, can be explained in understandable terms. Just remember this: *Do not be afraid to ask questions!*

I read that standardized tests aren't fair because all they really show is a child's social class. Is that true?

Some experts believe that a child's socioeconomic status (SES), which generally is defined by two words—*family income*—is related to proficiency test scores more than any other single factor—more than the quality of teachers, more than class size, and more than the amount of money allocated to schools.

This has been a major argument against standardized testing. It shows how the use of standardized tests has the potential to unfairly exclude many students from lower-income families from passing to the next grade, graduating from high school, or being admitted to a college of their choice. This strong relationship between test scores and family income is a compelling reason why we should use additional ways of evaluating students rather than relying so heavily on tests such as standardized proficiency tests.

Although the relationship between SES and school achievement/test scores is strong, that does not mean that poor children are destined to fail in school. Nor does it mean that they should give up hope of ever graduating from high school or attending college. In fact, a growing body of evidence suggests that children from poor backgrounds, when provided with the right instruction, can achieve at least as well as their wealthier peers. In his book, *Teach Like a Champion* (2010), Doug Lemov tells how specific teaching techniques implemented in several schools in New York and New Jersey have led to significant gains in achievement among disadvantaged children.

Why are tests relied on so much to make important decisions?

This has been one of the most asked questions and also one of the most persistent criticisms of tests. Stories of how the use of tests has led to illogical decisions are plentiful. In some instances, blind faith in tests guides decisions about our children, decisions that sometimes fly in the face of common sense. Whether it is a child with good grades being held back because of not passing a section of the proficiency test by a point or two, or a high school senior with an excellent GPA being denied admission to a particular college because of less than stellar scores on a college admissions test. In situations like these, blind faith appears to have driven common sense out of the decision-making process.

The roots of this blind reliance on tests can be found in society's belief in the "magic of numbers." There's a natural tendency to assume that because numbers are used in testing, it must mean that tests are precision instruments and, therefore, produce precise results. The use of complex statistical analyses does allow human characteristics to be measured in a scientific manner, but educational and psychological tests are far from being precision instruments. Consequently, test results are not exact measures of an individual's achievement skills, intelligence level, personality characteristics, or whatever it is that is being evaluated.

You may find that some school systems tend to treat test results as exact measures of a child's performance, but the results instead should be thought of as good *general* estimates. And that's only if you can be sure the student put forth an earnest effort to do well and was in reasonably good health when taking the test. Simple matters such as whether a child was motivated to do well on the test, or whether he or she had the flu bug at the time of the testing, can have a substantial adverse impact on the results.

DEFINITIONS

Achievement test: A type of test that measures academic skills, like spelling, arithmetic, and reading. It tells you how much a child has learned in each subject area.

Adaptive behavior: These are self-help or independent living skills needed to take care of oneself. They include skills like dressing, telling time, cooking, doing laundry, getting about in the community, and managing personal finances.

Age equivalent: This is the student's test score expressed in age levels (that is, years and months).

Anxiety: Unpleasant feelings of tension, fear, apprehension, or worry. (See also test anxiety.)

Asperger's disorder: A type of pervasive developmental disorder which is characterized mainly by problems in the development of social skills. Some experts consider Asperger's disorder to be a mild form of autism.

Audiologist: A professional who gives auditory (hearing) tests to determine a child's capacity to hear and whether hearing problems may be present.

Autism: A pervasive developmental disability that severely affects a child's ability to communicate and interact with others.

Bell curve: (See normal curve.)

Bias: An influence from the examiner that could affect the results of a testing. This could include things like prejudice or other partiality.

Confidence interval: A range of scores within which a person's "true score" falls.

Criterion-referenced tests: These are tests that measure what a child knows or can do in a specific school subject, such as math, science, or spelling, without comparison to his or her peers.

Curriculum-based measurement (CBM): A quick and effective way to assess a student's skill levels in areas such as reading fluency, spelling, math, and written expression. Unlike a norm-referenced test, which usually takes a considerable amount of time to administer and score, administering a CBM is quick (usually 1 to 5 minutes) and scoring is straightforward.

Depression: A mood disorder characterized by a persistently negative and pessimistic view of oneself, the world, and the future. Disruption of sleep and appetite, loss of interest in previously interesting activities, unhappiness, and lack of energy are just a few of the symptoms of depression.

Educational/learning specialist: A professional who administers educational tests, analyzes the test results, and recommends appropriate learning strategies.

Emotional intelligence: A concept proposed by Daniel Goleman which emphasizes that how we handle our emotions is as important in life as the traditional notion of IQ. In particular, things such as communicating effectively, being aware of and understanding our own feelings, understanding the views and feelings of others, how well we make decisions, how effectively we manage stress and conflict, insight, and social acuity are important elements that relate to success.

False negative: When the results of a test indicate that a person does not have a condition when they actually do have it.

False positive: When the results of a test indicate that a person has a condition when they really do not have it.

Genius: A word used to describe someone who is exceptionally intelligent, driven, extremely focused in a particular area of interest, determined, and inventive in thinking. A genius generally is someone who has made a major and lasting positive contribution to society. Examples of geniuses would be Isaac Newton, Albert Einstein, and Leonard da Vinci.

Grade equivalent: This is the student's test score expressed in grade levels.

Grade deflation: When teachers are stringent in their grading, resulting in grades that are lower than they would be normally.

Grade inflation: When teachers are lenient in their grading, resulting in grades that are higher than they would be normally.

Heritability: The degree to which a trait is inherited or passed on genetically.

High-stakes testing: When the results of a test or tests are used to make important decisions, such as to retain a child or to allow a student to graduate.

Inference: A logical conclusion. In the testing world, an inference is a logical conclusion based on testing results.

Intellectual disability: This is the newer term for mental retardation. It represents significantly below average intellectual functioning with significantly below average adaptive behavior (independent living skills) that occurs during childhood (18 years or younger).

Intelligence: A complex concept that includes a wide range of abilities. In particular, it relates to the ability to solve problems, to reason, and to understand the world in which we live.

Intelligence test: A standardized test that measures mental ability or intelligence/IQ.

IQ: This is what an intelligence test measures. IQ stands for Intelligence Quotient and is considered to represent a person's level of intelligence.

Learning disability: When a child has difficulty with learning and learns much less than expected, despite his or her best efforts. For example, a child of average intelligence who is failing several school subjects even though he is doing his homework and studying hard could have a learning disability.

Mean (average): The technical or statistical term for "average."

Mental retardation: (See intellectual disability.)

Multiple disabilities: When a child has two or more disabilities, for example, intellectual disability and deafness.

Multiple intelligence: This is a contemporary concept of intelligence which suggests that there actually are several types of intelligences operating in our lives rather than only one.

Norm: The average or "normal" performance of a group of individuals on a certain test.

Normal curve: This is the distribution of scores that has the shape of a bell (it's sometimes called the bell-shaped curve) where most scores fall in the middle (average) and the fewest scores are at the high and low ends.

Normal Curve Equivalent (NCE): Similar to a percentile rank but with equal intervals between scores. Although sometimes listed on computer-generated reports, the NCE is used primarily for research.

Norm-referenced tests: Standardized tests that compare a child's performance to their age or grade peers (norm group).

Objective test: A test that has standardized procedures for administration and scoring. Examples of objective tests are true/false and multiple choice tests.

Orthopedic impairment: A physical disability that interferes with walking, using one's arms and hands, or with other body movements.

Overachievement: The idea that a person is achieving more than what their ability level would suggest.

Percent (percentage): The number of questions answered correctly divided by the total number of questions on a test; commonly used with classroom tests.

Percentile (percentile rank): This score tells what percentage of students the examinee scored higher (or lower) than; commonly used with standardized tests.

Performance assessment: Performance assessment requires students to demonstrate their knowledge through practical activities rather than by answering multiple choice or true/false questions.

Personality: An individual's unique and enduring pattern of behavioral dispositions, thoughts, and feelings.

Personality test: A standardized test that measures one or more dimensions of a person's personality. Personality tests can be used to measure normal and abnormal behavior.

Portfolio assessment: When a student's classroom work is saved in a "portfolio," much like an artist or photographer saves their work. At the end of each grading period and the school year, the student's work is evaluated (using a scoring guide called a rubric) to see if progress has been made.

Proficiency test: (See achievement test.)

Projective personality tests (techniques): These are non-objective methods for measuring personality that use ambiguous stimuli. Examples are inkblots and drawing pictures.

Psychiatrist: A medical doctor/physician who specializes in treating psychiatric disorders. A psychiatrist may be an M.D. (Doctor of Medicine) or a D.O. (Doctor of Osteopathy).

Psychologist: A person, usually with a doctoral degree (and sometimes a master's degree) in psychology who studies human behavior. Among the many things a psychologist may do are psychotherapy, research, teaching, and psychological testing.

Raw score: A raw score is usually considered to be the number of questions on a test answered correctly.

Reliability: Reliability means that the person taking the test will get approximately the same results if he or she were tested again with the same or equivalent test.

Sampling: A part of a person's total behaviors or skills that accurately represents their total behaviors or skills.

Scaled score: A score that shows how far a person's score is from the average score of the norm group.

Serious emotional disturbance: An emotional or behavioral problem that significantly interferes with a child's ability to learn, to develop satisfactory relationships, and to function in routine day-to-day activities.

Specific learning disability: A learning problem that interferes with a child's ability to use language, think, listen, read, write, spell, or do math.

Speech/language pathologist: A professional who evaluates for speech and language problems and helps to remediate such problems.

Standard deviation: The standard deviation is a measure of the dispersion of a set of scores from the average (also called the mean); it tells us how far the scores are spread out.

Standard score: A type of score that tells us how far a person's score is from the average score of the norm group.

Standardized test: A test that is administered according standard rules, is scored objectively, and uses norms.

Stress: Events in our life that disrupt or threaten to disrupt our physical or emotional well-being.

Test: A test is set of standard procedures for measuring a sampling (that is, only a part) of a person's behaviors or skills.

Test anxiety (also called test-taking anxiety): Extreme nervousness and tension when taking tests that can interfere with test performance and cause the child's test scores to be lower than what the child is capable of scoring.

Test battery: A group of tests used to evaluate an individual.

Test item: This is the same thing as a test question.

Test sophistication: The ability to do relatively well on tests, often standardized achievement/proficiency tests, even though the person may not be adequately prepared or know the material well.

T-score: A type of standard score often used with personality tests. Like other standard scores, the T-Score tells you whether a score is below average, average, or above average.

Underachievement: When a child is achieving at a level lower than he or she is capable of achieving.

Validity: Validity means that a test measures what it was designed to measure.

Zone of Proximal Development (ZPD): This is a child's "comfort zone" of reading. The ZPD is reported as a grade-level range. Grade levels within the range are considered to be appropriate for the student's reading level.

APPENDIX

Commonly Used Tests

What follows are basic descriptions of a sampling of tests sometimes used to evaluate children. The list is for informational and educational purposes only and is not intended to be used as a menu from which parents or teachers select or recommend a particular test. Test selection should be done only by qualified professionals.

A listing here does not imply sponsorship, affiliation, or endorsement by the test publishers of any products or services of Rocklin Publications or the author, including the content of *GET SMART ABOUT TESTS*. Also, a listing here does not imply sponsorship, affiliation, or endorsement of the products or services of the test publishers by Rocklin Publications or the author. Aside from the author having used many of the tests on a professional basis, neither Rocklin Publications nor the author has any relationship with any of the test publishers listed.

You will notice that a pronunciation for the test's acronym is provided for some of the tests. This is done because professionals, when discussing tests or scores, often refer to the test's acronym rather than the formal name of the test. For example, the acronym for the Wechsler Intelligence Scale for Children-4th Edition is WISC-IV (pronounced "WISK-4)," and the acronym for the Wide Range Achievement Test-4th Edition is WRAT-4 (pronounced "RAT-4"). So a psychologist might say, "I administered the WISC-IV and WRAT-4 to Sally today." Now when you hear professionals use this cryptic language, at least you'll have some idea of what they're talking about. Of course, you can't be expected to know what every acronym stands for, so it's always a good idea to ask.

Lastly, the tests listed here are for English-speaking children. For some tests, Spanish editions also are available.

Achievement/Proficiency Tests

AIMSweb
Published by: The Psychological Corporation/Pearson
Type: A series of short (1-3 minutes), standardized curriculum-based tests that are individually administered.
What's it used for: To screen students in areas such as reading comprehension, math, early literacy, and written expression; also used to monitor the progress of children identified as "at risk" and who are receiving educational interventions.
Age/grade range: Grades K through 8.
Time to administer: 1-3 minutes per test, or approximately 10-15 minutes per student, depending on the tests administered.

Dynamic Indicators of Basic Early Literacy Skills (DIBELS)
Published by: University of Oregon Center on Teaching and Learning
Type: A series of short (1-3 minutes), standardized curriculum-based tests that are individually administered.
What's it used for: To screen students in early literacy skills, such as letter-naming fluency and oral reading fluency; also used to monitor the progress of children identified as "at risk" and who are receiving educational interventions.
Age/grade range: Grades K through 8.
Time to administer: 1-3 minutes per test, or approximately 10 minutes per student, depending on the tests administered.

Iowa Tests of Basic Skills (ITBS)
by H.D. Hoover, S.B. Dunbar, & D.A. Frisbie
Published by: Riverside Publishing
Type: Group-administered.
What's it used for: As a comprehensive measure of reading, language arts, mathematics, social studies, science, and sources of information (such as reading maps and diagrams).
Age/grade range: Grades K through 8.
Time to administer: Several hours; administered over days.

Kaufman Test of Educational Achievement, Second Edition (KTEA–II)

by Alan S. Kaufman & Nadeen L. Kaufman
Published by: Pearson
Type: Individually administered.
What's it used for: To assess academic achievement skills.
Age/grade range: 4 years-6 months through 25 years for comprehensive form or 4 years-6 months through 90+ years for brief form.
Time to administer: Approximately 15-80 minutes, depending on individual's age and form used.

KeyMath 3 Diagnostic Assessment

by Austin J. Connolly
Published by: Pearson
Type: Individually administered.
What's it used for: To measure math concepts and skills.
Age/grade range: 4 years-6 months through 22 years; grades K through 12.
Time to administer: Approximately 30-90 minutes.

Metropolitan Achievement Tests–Eighth Edition

Published by: The Psychological Corporation/Pearson
Type: Group-administered.
What's it used for: To assess educational achievement skills in reading, mathematics, language arts, science, and social studies.
Age/grade range: Grades K through 12.
Time to administer: Varies; approximately 1½ to 4 hours for complete battery, depending on grade of student.

Peabody Individual Achievement Test–Revised/ Normative Update (PIAT–R/NU)

by Frederick C. Markwardt, Jr.
Published by: Pearson
Pronounced: PEA-OTT
Type: Individually administered.
What's it used for: To measure academic achievement skills.
Age/grade range: 5 years through 22 years.
Time to administer: Approximately 60 minutes.

Peabody Picture Vocabulary Test, Fourth Edition (PPVT–4)
by Lloyd M. Dunn & Douglas M. Dunn
Published by: Pearson
Type: Individually administered.
What's it used for: To measure listening comprehension/hearing vocabulary; can be used with non-English speaking students because reading is not required.
Age/grade range: 2 years-6 months through 90+ years.
Time to administer: Approximately 15 minutes.

Stanford Achievement Test Series
Published by: The Psychological Corporation/Pearson
Type: Group-administered.
What's it used for: To assess educational achievement skills.
Age/grade range: Grades K through 12.
Time to administer: Varies.

Tests of Achievement and Proficiency (TAP)
by Dale P. Scannell, Oscar M. Haugh, Brenda H. Loyd,
& C. Frederick Risinger
Published by: Riverside Publishing
Type: Group-administered.
What's it used for: To assess students' academic progress in high school.
Age/grade range: Grades 9 through 12.
Time to administer: Four hours and 15 minutes for complete battery; 90 minutes for survey battery.

Test of Early Reading Ability–Deaf or Hard of Hearing (TERA–D/HH)
by D. Kim Reid, Wayne P. Hresko, Donald D. Hammill, & Susan Wiltshire
Published by: PRO-ED
Type: Individually administered.
What it's used for: To assess reading skills in children with moderate to profound hearing loss.
Age/grade range: 3 years through 13 years.
Time to administer: Approximately 20-30 minutes.

Test of Early Reading Ability, Third Edition (TERA–3)
by D. Kim Reid, Wayne P. Hresko, & Donald D. Hammill
Published by: PRO-ED
Type: Individually administered.
What's it used for: To assess early reading skills.
Age/grade range: 3 years-6 months through 8 years-6 months.
Time to administer: Approximately 30 minutes.

Wechsler Individual Achievement Test–Third Edition (WIAT–III)
by David Wechsler
Published by: The Psychological Corporation/Pearson
Type: Individually administered
What's it used for: To measure academic achievement skills.
Age/grade range: 4 years through 50 years-11 months.
Time to administer: Varies; depends on child's grade level and on how many subtests are administered.

Wide Range Achievement Test–Fourth Edition (WRAT–4)
by Gary S. Wilkinson & Gary J. Robertson
Published by: Psychological Assessment Resources
Pronounced: RAT-4
Type: Individual or group administration.
What's it used for: To measure academic achievement skills.
Age/grade range: 5 years through adult.
Time to administer: Approximately 15-45 minutes.

Woodcock-Johnson III Normative Update (NU) Tests of Achievement
by Richard W. Woodcock , Kevin S. McGrew, & Nancy Mather
Published by: Riverside Publishing
Type: Individually administered.
What's it used for: To assess oral language and academic achievement skills.
Age/grade range: 2 years through 90+.
Time to administer: Approximately 60-70 minutes.

Adaptive Behavior Scales

Adaptive Behavior Assessment System–Second Edition (ABAS–II)
by Patti L. Harrison & Thomas Oakland
Published by: The Psychological Corporation/Pearson
Type: Checklist completed by parent, caregiver, teacher, or daycare personnel.
What it's used for: To assess self-help/independent living skills.
Age/grade range: Birth to 89 years-11 months.
Time to administer: Approximately 15-20 minutes.

AAMR Adaptive Behavior Scales–School: Second Edition
by Nadine Lambert, Kazuo Nihira, & Henry Leland
Published by: PRO-ED
Type: Interview format. Completed by person who interviews parent or other person who knows the child well.
What it's used for: To assess self-help/independent living skills.
Age/grade range: 3 years through 18 years.
Time to administer: Approximately 15-30 minutes.

AAMR Adaptive Behavior Scales–Residential and Community: Second Edition
by Kazuo Nihira, Henry Leland, & Nadine Lambert
Published by: PRO-ED
Type: Interview format. Completed by person who interviews parent or other person who knows the child well.
What it's used for: To assess self-help/independent living skills.
Age/grade range: 18 years through 80 years.
Time to administer: Approximately 15-30 minutes.

Vineland Adaptive Behavior Scales, Second Edition (Vineland II)
by Sara S. Sparrow, Dominic V. Cicchetti, & David A. Ballo
Published by: Pearson
Type: Interview format. Completed by person who interviews parent or other person who knows the child well; teacher rating form also available.
What it's used for: To assess self-help/independent living skills of individuals with special needs, such as individuals with mental retardation and autism.
Age/grade range: Birth through 90 years.
Time to administer: Approximately 20-60 minutes.

Behavior Screening Tests

Attention Deficit Disorders Evaluation Scale–Third Edition (AD-DES-3)

by Stephen B. McCarney

Published by: Hawthorne Educational Services

Type: Home and school forms for ages School form for education personnel and Home form for parents.

What it's used for: To aid in the assessment of attention-deficit/hyperactivity disorder (ADHD)

Age/grade range: 4 years through 18 years.

Time to administer: Approximately 12 to 15 minutes, depending on form used.

Beck Anxiety Inventory (BAI)

by Aaron T. Beck

Published by: The Psychological Corporation/Pearson

Type: Self-report.

What it's used for: To assess anxiety.

Age/grade range: 17 years to 80 years.

Time to administer: Approximately 5-10 minutes.

Beck Depression Inventory–II (BDI–II)

by Aaron T. Beck, Robert A. Steer, & Gregory K. Brown

Published by: The Psychological Corporation/Pearson

Type: Self-report.

What it's used for: To assess depression.

Age/grade range: 13 years to 80 years.

Time to administer: Approximately 5-10 minutes.

Beck Hopelessness Scale (BHS)

by Aaron T. Beck

Published by: The Psychological Corporation/Pearson

Type: Self-report.

What it's used for: To assess hopelessness; can be helpful in assessing for suicidal ideation and intent.

Age/grade range: 17 years to 80 years.

Time to administer: Approximately 5-10 minutes.

Beck Youth Inventories–Second Edition

by Judith S. Beck, Aaron T. Beck, & John B. Jolly
Published by: The Psychological Corporation/Pearson
Type: Self-report.
What it's used for: To assess depression, anxiety, anger, disruptive behavior, and self-concept.
Age/grade range: 7 years through 18 years.
Time to administer: Approximately 15-20 minutes.

Brown Attention–Deficit Disorder Scales (Brown ADD Scales)

by Thomas E. Brown
Published by: The Psychological Corporation/Pearson
Type: Parent and teacher questionnaires for ages 3 to 12 years; self-report for ages 8 years through adult.
What it's used for: To screen for attention-deficit disorder (ADD) and attention-deficit/hyperactivity disorder (ADHD).
Age/grade range: 3 years through adult.
Time to administer: Approximately 10-20 minutes

Children's Depression Inventory (CDI)

by Maria Kovacs
Published by: Multi-Health Systems
Type: Completed by the child (self-report) and also by parent and teacher.
What it's used for: To assess symptoms of depression in children and adolescents.
Age/grade range: 7 years to 17 years.
Time to administer: Approximately 5-15 minutes.

Children's Measure of Obsessive-Compulsive Symptoms (CMOCS)

by Cecil R. Reynolds & Ronald B. Livingston
Published by: Western Psychological Services
Type: Completed by the child (self-report).
What it's used for: To assess symptoms of obsessive-compulsive disorder (OCD) in children and adolescents.
Age/grade range: 8 years to 19 years.
Time to administer: Approximately 10-15 minutes.

Conners 3rd Edition (Conners 3)
by C. Keith Conners
Published by: Multi-Health Systems
Type: Parent and teacher forms for ages 6 to 18 years; self-report for ages 8 to 18 years.
What it's used for: Measures several dimensions of a child's behavior; often used to screen for attention-deficit disorder (ADD) and attention-deficit/hyperactivity disorder (ADHD).
Age/grade range: 6 years to 18 years.
Time to administer: Approximately 20 minutes.

Devereux Behavior Rating Scale–School Form
by Jack A. Naglieri, Paul A. LeBuffe, & Steven I. Pfeiffer
Published by: The Psychological Corporation/Pearson
Type: Completed by child's parent or teacher.
What it's used for: Used to measure four basic dimensions of a child's behavior; can be helpful in screening for emotional problems.
Age/grade range: 5 years to 18 years.
Time to administer: Approximately 5 minutes.

Piers–Harris Children's Self-Concept Scale, Second Edition (Piers–Harris 2)
by Ellen V. Piers, Dale B. Harris, & David S. Herzberg
Published by: Western Psychological Services
Type: Completed by child (self-report).
What it's used for: To assess self-concept in children.
Age/grade range: 7 years to 18 years
Time to administer: Approximately 10-15 minutes.

Reynolds Adolescent Depression Scale–Second Edition (RADS-2)
by William M. Reynolds
Published by: Psychological Assessment Resources
Pronounced: RADS-2 (rhymes with dads-2).
Type: Self-report.
What it's used for: To screen for adolescent depression.
Age/grade range: 13 years through 18 years.
Time to administer: Approximately 5-10 minutes.

Vanderbilt ADHD Diagnostic Rating Scales
by Mark L. Wolraich
Published by: In the public domain; available at various Web sites.
Type: Separate forms completed by parent and teacher.
What it's used for: To screen for attention-deficit/hyperactivity disorder (ADHD); often used by pediatricians.
Age/grade range: 6 years through 12 years.
Time to administer: Approximately 10 minutes.

Career Interest Inventories

Career Assessment Inventory (CAI)
by Charles B. Johansson
Published by: Pearson
Type: Self-administered; individual or group administration.
What it's used for: Career/vocational guidance. Enhanced version—for persons with four years of post-secondary/college training. Vocational version—for persons considering non-college, business, or technical college careers.
Age/grade range: 15 years and older.
Time to administer: Approximately 40 minutes.

Kuder Career Planning System
by Frederick Kuder
Published by: Kuder, Inc.
Type: Self-administered; Internet/online system.
What it's used for: Vocational guidance and career planning.
Age/grade range: Middle school students to adults.
Time to administer: Varies.

Reading-Free Vocational Interest Inventory: 2 (RVII: 2)
by Ralph L. Becker
Published by: Elbern Publications
Type: Self-administered; individual or group administration.
What it's used for: Career guidance; measures vocational interests of persons with special needs, such as those with an intellectual disability.
Age/grade range: 13 years and older.
Time to administer: Approximately 20 minutes.

Self Directed Search
by John L. Holland
Published by: Psychological Assessment Resources
Type: Self-administered; individual or group administration.
What it's used for: Career/vocational guidance.
Age/grade range: High school and college students; adults.
Time to administer: Approximately 35-45 minutes, depending on which form is used.

Strong Interest Inventory and Skills Confidence Inventory
Nancy E. Betz, Fred H. Borgen, &Lenore W. Harmon
Published by: Consulting Psychologists Press
Type: Self-administered; individual or group administration.
What it's used for: Career/vocational guidance; self-assurance about careers.
Age/grade range: Adolescents and adults.
Time to administer: Approximately 40-50 minutes.

College Admissions Tests

ACT
Published by: ACT, Inc.
Type: Group-administered.
What it's used for: College admissions.
Age/grade range: High school juniors and seniors.
Time to administer: Two hours and 55 minutes; add 30 minutes for essay.

Preliminary SAT (PSAT)
Published by: The College Board
Type: Group-administered.
What it's used for: Practice for the SAT; to aid in determining eligibility for a National Merit Scholarship.
Age/grade range: Typically given to high school sophomores.
Time to administer: Two hours and 10 minutes.

SAT
Published by: The College Board
Type: Group-administered.
What it's used for: College admissions.
Age/grade range: High school juniors and seniors.
Time to administer: Three hours and 45 minutes.

Developmental Disorders Tests

Asperger Syndrome Diagnostic Scale (ASDS)
by Brenda Myles, Stacey Bock, & Richard Simpson
Published by: PRO-ED
Type: Completed by parents and professionals.
What it's used for: To assess for Asperger's syndrome.
Age/grade range: 2 years through 18 years.
Time to administer: Approximately 10-15 minutes.

Autistic Spectrum Rating Scales (ASRS)
by Sam Goldstein & Jack A. Naglieri
Published by: Multi-Health Systems
Type: Completed by parents or teachers.
What it's used for: Helps to identify symptoms and behaviors associated with autism spectrum disorders.
Age/grade range: 2 years through 18 years.
Time to administer: Approximately 20 minutes.

Childhood Autism Rating Scale, 2nd Edition (CARS2)
by Eric Schopler, Mary E. Van Bourgondien, Glenna Janette Wellman, & Steven R. Love, Ph.D
Published by: Western Psychological Services
Type: Completed by examiner.
What it's used for: To screen for autism.
Age/grade range: 2 years and up.
Time to administer: Approximately 5-10 minutes.

Gilliam Asperger's Disorder Scale (GADS)
by James E. Gilliam
Published by: PRO-ED
Type: Completed by parents and professionals.
What it's used for: To screen for Asperger's disorder.
Age/grade range: 3 years through 22 years.
Time to administer: Approximately 5-10 minutes.

Gilliam Autism Rating Scale, Second Edition (GARS–2)
by James E. Gilliam
Published by: PRO-ED
Type: Completed by parents and professionals.
What it's used for: To screen for autism.
Age/grade range: 3 years through 22 years.
Time to administer: 5-10 minutes.

Pervasive Developmental Disorders Screening Test–II
by Bryna Siegel
Published by: The Psychological Corporation/Pearson
Type: Completed by parents and professionals.
What it's used for: To screen for autism and Asperger's disorder..
Age/grade range: 1 year-6 months through 4 years.
Time to administer: Approximately 10-20 minutes.

Intelligence Tests

Baley Scales of Infant and Toddler Development–Third Edition
by Nancy Baley
Published by: The Psychological Corporation/Pearson
Type: Individually administered.
What's it used for: To assess intellectual, motor, language, adaptive behavior, and emotional development.
Age/grade range: 1 month through 42 months.
Time to administer: Approximately 30-60 minutes.

Cognitive Abilities Test (CogAT)
by David F. Lohman & Elizabeth P. Hagen
Published by: Riverside Publishing
Type: Group administered.
What's it used for: To assess cognitive (intellectual) abilities in reasoning and problem solving.
Age/grade range: Grades K through 12.
Time to administer: Varies depending on grade; approximately 30-60 minutes. (NOTE: The CogAT typically is administered with the Iowa Tests of Basic Skills and the Tests of Achievement and Proficiency. *See under Achievement/Proficiency Tests.*)

Columbia Mental Maturity Scale
by Bessie B. Burgemeister, Lucille Hollander Blum, & Irving Lorge
Published by: The Psychological Corporation/Pearson
Type: Individually administered.
What's it used for: To assess mental ability; requires no verbal responses and minimal motor responses.
Age/grade range: 3 years-6 months through 9 years.
Time to administer: Approximately 15-20 minutes.

Comprehensive Test of Nonverbal Intelligence (CTONI)
by Donald D. Hammill, Nils A. Pearson, & J. Lee Wiederholt
Published by: PRO-ED
Pronounced: C-TONI (or See Tony)
Type: Individually administered.
What it's used for: To assess nonverbal intellectual functioning; does not require the use of language.
Age/grade range: 6 years through 90 years.
Time to administer: Approximately 60 minutes.

Das • Naglieri Cognitive Assessment System (CAS)
by Jack A. Naglieri & J.P. Das
Published by: Riverside Publishing
Type: Individually administered.
What it's used for: To assess children's cognitive ability with minimal influence from culture.
Age/grade range: 5 years through 17 years.
Time to administer: Approximately 40 minutes for basic battery to 60 minutes for standard battery.

Detroit Tests of Learning Aptitude–Fourth Edition
by Donald D. Hammill
Published by: PRO-ED
Type: Individually administered.
What it's used for: To assess general intelligence and specific abilities.
Age/grade range: 6 years through 17 years.
Time to administer: Approximately 40 minutes to 2 hours.

Detroit Tests of Learning Aptitude–Primary: Third Edition
by Donald D. Hammill & Brian R. Bryant
Published by: PRO-ED
Type: Individually administered.
What it's used for: To assess general intelligence of young children.
Age/grade range: 3 years through 9 years.
Time to administer: Approximately 15-45 minutes.

Differential Ability Scales–Second Edition (DAS-II)
by Colin D. Elliott
Published by: The Psychological Corporation/Pearson
Type: Individually administered.
What it's used for: To assess cognitive abilities of children and adolescents.
Age/grade range: 2 years-6 months through 17 years.
Time to administer: Approximately 45-60 minutes.

Kaufman Assessment Battery for Children, Second Edition (KABC–II)
by Alan S. Kaufman & Nadeen L. Kaufman
Published by: Pearson
Type: Individually administered.
What's it used for: To assess intellectual functioning.
Age/grade range: 3 through 18 years.
Time to administer: Approximately 25-70 minutes.

Kaufman Brief Intelligence Test, Second Edition (KBIT–2)
by Alan S. Kaufman & Nadeen L. Kaufman
Published by: Pearson
Type: Individually administered.
What's it used for: To provide a quick estimate of intellectual functioning; not to be used to make placement decisions.
Age/grade range: 4 through 90 years.
Time to administer: Approximately 20 minutes.

Naglieri Nonverbal Ability Test (NNAT)–Individual Administration
by Jack A. Naglieri
Published by: The Psychological Corporation/Pearson
Type: Individually administered.
What's it used for: To assess nonverbal reasoning abilities independent of a child's language or cultural background.
Age/grade range: 5 through 17 years.
Time to administer: Approximately 25-30 minutes.

Primary Test of Nonverbal Intelligence (PTONI)
by David J. Ehrler & Ronnie L. McGhee
Published by: PRO-ED
Type: Individually administered.
What it's used for: To assess nonverbal intellectual functioning; does not require the use of language or English-speaking skills.
Age/grade range: 3 years through 9 years.
Time to administer: Approximately 5-15 minutes.

Raven's Progressive Matrices
by J.C. Raven
Published by: The Psychological Corporation/Pearson
Type: Individual and group administration.
What's it used for: Nonverbal measure of intelligence.
Age/grade range: 5 years to adult, depending on level and form used.
Time to administer: Approximately 15-60 minutes, depending on level and form used.

Reynolds Intellectual Assessment Scales (RIAS)
by Cecil R. Reynolds & Randy W. Kamphaus
Published by: Psychological Assessment Resources
Type: Individually administered.
What it's used for: Assessment of intellectual functioning in children and adults; includes supplemental measure of memory.
Age/grade range: 3 years to 94 years.
Time to administer: Approximately 20-35 minutes.

Slosson Intelligence Test-Revised (SIT–R3)
by Richard L. Slosson, Revised by Charles L. Nicholson
& Terry L. Hibpshman
Published by: Slosson Educational Publications
Type: Individually administered.
What's it used for: Screening for intellectual functioning; not recommended for placement decisions.
Age/grade range: 4 years to 65 years.
Time to administer: Approximately 10-30 minutes.

Stanford-Binet Intelligence Scales for Early Childhood (Early SB5)
by Gale H. Roid
Published by: Riverside Publishing
Type: Individually administered.
What's it used for: To assess intellectual functioning in early childhood.
Age/grade range: 2 years through 5 years for full battery; 6 years to 7 years-3 months for abbreviated battery.
Time to administer: Approximately 30-50 minutes for full battery; 15-20 minutes for abbreviated batter.

Stanford-Binet Intelligence Scales, Fifth Edition (SB5)
by Gale H. Roid
Published by: Riverside Publishing
Type: Individually administered.
What's it used for: To assess intellectual functioning.
Age/grade range: 2 years to 85 years+.
Time to administer: Approximately 60-75 minutes.

Test of Nonverbal Intelligence, Fourth Edition (TONI–4)
by Linda Brown, Rita J. Sherbenou, & Susan K. Johnsen
Published by: PRO-ED
Pronounced: TONI-4 (rhymes with Tony)
Type: Individually administered.
What it's used for: To assess intellectual functioning; does not require the use of language.
Age/grade range: 6 years through 89 years.
Time to administer: Approximately 15-20 minutes.

Wechsler Abbreviated Scale of Intelligence (WASI)
by David Wechsler
Published by: The Psychological Corporation/Pearson
Type: Individually administered.
What it's used for: A brief measure of intellectual functioning.
Age/grade range: 6 years through 89 years.
Time to administer: 15-30 minutes.

Wechsler Adult Intelligence Scale–Fourth Edition (WAIS–IV)
by David Wechsler
Published by: The Psychological Corporation/Pearson
Pronounced: WACE-4 (rhymes with pace)
Type: Individually administered.
What it's used for: To assess intellectual functioning.
Age/grade range: 16 years through 90 years.
Time to administer: Approximately 60-90 minutes.

Wechsler Intelligence Scale for Children–Fourth Edition (WISC–IV)
by David Wechsler
Published by: The Psychological Corporation/Pearson
Pronounced: WISK-4
Type: Individually administered.
What it's used for: To assess intellectual functioning.
Age/grade range: 6 years through 16 years.
Time to administer: Approximately 75 minutes.

Wechsler Nonverbal Scale of Ability (WNV)
by David Wechsler & Jack A. Naglieri
Published by: The Psychological Corporation/Pearson
Type: Individually administered.
What it's used for: To assess intellectual functioning; does not require the use of language; useful for culturally diverse groups.
Age/grade range: 4 years through 21 years.
Time to administer: Approximately 15-45 minutes.

Wechsler Preschool and Primary Scale of Intelligence–Third Edition (WPPSI–III)
by David Wechsler
Published by: The Psychological Corporation/Pearson
Pronounced: WIPSEE-3
Type: Individually administered.
What it's used for: To assess intellectual functioning; when developmental delays are suspected.
Age/grade range: 2 years-6 months to 7 years-3 months.
Time to administer: Approximately 30-60 minutes.

Woodcock–Johnson III Tests of Cognitive Abilities
by Richard W. Woodcock , Kevin S. McGrew, & Nancy Mather
Published by: Riverside Publishing
Type: Individually administered.
What's it used for: To measure cognitive/intellectual abilities.
Age/grade range: 2 years to 90 years+.
Time to administer: Approximately 50-60 minutes.

Language & Reading Tests

Clinical Evaluation of Language Fundamentals–Fourth Edition (CELF–4)
by Eleanor Semel, Elisabeth H. Wiig, and Wayne A. Secord
Published by: The Psychological Corporation/Pearson
Pronounced: SELF-4
Type: Individually administered.
What it's used for: To assess language performance.
Age/grade range: 5 years through 21 years.
Time to administer: Approximately 30-60 minutes.

Comprehensive Test of Phonological Processing (CTOPP)
by Richard Wagner, Joseph Torgesen, and Carol Rashotte
Published by: PRO-ED
Type: Individually administered.
What it's used for: To assess phonological skills to aid in determining the presence of a reading disability.
Age/grade range: 5 years through 24 years.
Time to administer: Approximately 30 minutes.

Goldman–Fristoe Test of Articulation 2
by Ronald Goldman & Macalyne Fristoe
Published by: Pearson
Type: Self-administered.
What it's used for: To screen for receptive and expressive language problems.
Age/grade range: 2 years through 21 years.
Time to administer: Varies per section.

Gray Oral Reading Tests–Fourth Edition (GORT–4)
by J. Lee Wiederholt & Brian R. Bryant
Published by: PRO-ED
Type: Individually administered.
What's it used for: To measure oral reading and to help determine oral reading problems.
Age/grade range: 6 years through 18 years.
Time to administer: Approximately 20-30 minutes.

Gray Diagnostic Reading Tests–Second Edition (GDRT–2)
by Brian R. Bryant, J. Lee Weiderholt, & Diane Pedrotty Bryant
Published by: PRO-ED
Type: Individually administered.
What's it used for: To provide comprehensive measures of reading strengths and weakness and to help determine reading problems.
Age/grade range: 6 years through 13 years.
Time to administer: Approximately 45-60 minutes.

Test of Early Language Development–Third Edition (TELD–3)
by Wayne Hresko, D. Kim Reid, & Donald D. Hammill
Published by: PRO-ED
Type: Self-administered.
What it's used for: To screen for receptive and expressive language problems.
Age/grade range: 2 years through 7 years.
Time to administer: Approximately 20 minutes.

Test of Phonological Awareness–Second Edition: Plus (TOPA–2+)
by Joseph K. Torgensen & Brian R. Bryant
Published by: PRO-ED
Type: Individual or group administered.
What it's used for: To screen for phonological problems.
Age/grade range: 5 years through 8 years.
Time to administer: Approximately 15-45 minutes.

Test of Written Language–Fourth Edition (TOWL–4)
by Donald D. Hammill & Stephen C. Larsen
Published by: PRO-ED
Type: Individual or group.
What it's used for: To assess written language/written expression skills.
Age/grade range: 9 years through 17 years.
Time to administer: Approximately 60-90 minutes.

Test of Early Written Language–Second Edition (TEWL–2)
by Wayne Hresko, Shelley Herron, & Pamela Peak
Published by: PRO-ED
Type: Self-administered.
What it's used for: To assess writing skills such as spelling, capitalization, punctuation, sentence construction, story construction.
Age/grade range: 4 years through 10 years.
Time to administer: Approximately 50 minutes.

Woodcock Reading Mastery Tests–Revised/Normative Update
by Richard W. Woodcock
Published by: Pearson
Type: Individually administered.
What it's used for: To assess reading readiness, basic reading skills, and word/passage comprehension.
Age/grade range: 5 years through 75+ years.
Time to administer: Approximately 10-30 minutes per cluster of tests.

Memory Tests

Children's Memory Scale (CMS)
by Morris Cohen
Published by: Pearson
Type: Individually administered.
What it's used for: To assess various aspects of memory in children.
Age/grade range: 5 years to 16 years.
Time to administer: Approximately 30 minutes.

Test of Memory and Learning, Second Edition (TOMAL–2)
by Cecil R. Reynolds and Judith K. Voress
Published by: PRO-ED
Type: Individually administered.
What it's used for: To assess various aspects of memory; sometimes used as part of a neuropsychological evaluation.
Age/grade range: 5 years through 59 years.
Time to administer: Approximately 30 minutes for core battery; 60 minutes if supplementary tests are administered.

Wechsler Memory Scale–Fourth Edition (WMS–IV)
by David Wechsler
Published by: Pearson
Type: Individually administered.
What it's used for: To assess memory functions; often used as part of a neuropsychological evaluation.
Age/grade range: 16 years through 90 years.
Time to administer: Approximately 30 minutes.

Wide Range Assessment of Memory and Learning, Second Edition (WRAML2)
by David Sheslow & Wayne Adams
Published by: Psychological Assessment Resources
Type: Individually administered.
What it's used for: To assess memory functions and learning; may be used as part of a neuropsychological evaluation.
Age/grade range: 5 years through 90 years.
Time to administer: Approximately 1 hour or less for core battery.

Personality Tests

Behavior Assessment System for Children–Second Edition (BASC–2)
by Cecil R. Reynolds & Randy W. Kamphaus
Published by: Pearson
Type: Parent and teacher ratings; self-report.
What it's used for: Comprehensive assessment used to evaluate children and young adults along several dimensions of behavioral and emotional functioning.
Age/grade range: 2 years to 21 years for teacher and parent scales; 8 years to college for self-report.
Time to administer: Approximately 10-20 minutes for parent and teacher forms; 30 minutes for self-report.

Millon Adolescent Clinical Inventory (MACI)
by Theodore Millon, Carrie Millon, & Roger Davis
Published by: Pearson
Type: Self-administered.
What it's used for: To assess emotional, behavioral, and interpersonal difficulties; personality assessment.
Age/grade range: 13 years to 19 years.
Time to administer: Approximately 30 minutes.

Millon Clinical Multiaxial Inventory–III (MCMI–III)
by Theodore Million, Carrie Millon, & Roger Davis
Published by: Pearson
Type: Self-administered.
What it's used for: To assess emotional, behavioral, and interpersonal difficulties; personality assessment.
Age/grade range: 18 years and older.
Time to administer: Approximately 30 minutes.

Minnesota Multiphasic Personality Inventory–Adolescent (MMPI–A)
by S.R. Hathaway & J.C. McKinley, & James N. Butcher,
John R. Graham, Carolyn L. Williams, & Beverly Kaemmer
Published by: University of Minnesota Press; distributed by Pearson
Type: Self-administered.
What it's used for: A comprehensive test that measures several dimensions of an adolescent's personality; helpful in determining emotional difficulties.
Age/grade range: 14 years through 17 years.
Time to administer: Approximately 45-60 minutes.

Minnesota Multiphasic Personality Inventory–2 (MMPI–2)
by S.R. Hathaway & J.C. McKinley and the MMPI Restandardization Committee of The University of Minnesota Press: James N. Butcher, W. Grant Dahlstrom, John R. Graham, & Auke Tellegen.
Published by: University of Minnesota Press; distributed by Pearson
Type: Self-administered.
What it's used for: A comprehensive test that measures several dimensions of personality; helpful in determining emotional difficulties.
Age/grade range: 18 years and older.
Time to administer: Approximately 60-90 minutes.

Myers-Briggs Type Indicator (MBTI)
by Isabel Briggs Myers & Katherine Briggs
Published by: Consulting Psychologists Press
Type: Individual or group administration.
What it's used for: Personal and career decisions; assesses normal behavior to help a person learn about him- or herself and how they relate to others.
Age/grade range: 14 years to adult.
Time to administer: Approximately 20-30 minutes.

Personality Assessment Inventory–Adolescent (PAI–A)
by Leslie C. Morey
Published by: Psychological Assessment Resources
Type: Individual or group administered.
What it's used for: Assessment of adolescent personality; helpful in determining emotional difficulties.
Age/grade range: 12 years to 18 years.
Time to administer: Approximately 30-45 minutes.

Personality Inventory for Children (PIC)
by Robert D. Wirt, David Lachar, James Klinedinst, & Phillip D. Seat
Published by: Western Psychological Services
Type: Completed by parent or adult who knows the child well.
What it's used for: A comprehensive test that measures several dimensions of a child's personality; helpful in determining emotional difficulties.
Age/grade range: 3 years through 16 years.
Time to administer: Approximately 45-90 minutes.

Projective Personality Tests (Techniques)

Children's Apperception Test (CAT)
by Leopold Bellak and Sonya Bellak
Published by: C.P.S., Inc.
Type: Individually administered.
What it's used for: To assess personality dynamics; perception of interpersonal relationships.
Age/grade range: 3 years through 10 years.
Time to administer: Varies.

Draw A Person: Screening Procedure for Emotional Disturbance
by Jack A. Naglieri, Timothy J. McNeish, Achilles N. Bardos
Published by: The Psychological Corporation/Pearson
Type: Individually administered.
What it's used for: To screen for emotional and behavioral disorders.
Age/grade range: 6 years through 17 years.
Time to administer: Approximately 15 minutes.

House–Tree–Person
by John N. Buck
Published by: Western Psychological Services
Type: Individually administered.
What it's used for: To assess personality dynamics.
Age/grade range: 3 years to adult.
Time to administer: Varies.

Rorschach Psychodiagnostics
by Hermann Rorschach
Published by: Hans Huber; distributed in U.S. by Grune & Stratton
Pronounced: Roar-shock.
Type: Individually administered.
What it's used for: To assess personality dynamics.
Age/grade range: 3 years to adult.
Time to administer: Varies.

Rotter Incomplete Sentences Blank, Second Edition
by Julian B. Rotter, Michael I. Lah, & Janet E. Rafferty
Published by: The Psychological Corporation/Pearson
Type: Individually administered.
What it's used for: To assess how child perceives self, others, and the world.
Age/grade range: High school to adult.
Time to administer: Approximately 20-40 minutes.

School Readiness &
Early Development Tests

Battelle Developmental Inventory, Second Edition (BDI–2)
by Jean Newborg
Published by: Riverside Publishing
Type: Individually administered.
What it's used for: To assess personal-social functioning, adaptive behaviors, motor and communication skills, and general cognitive ability; can be used for screening and to aid with diagnosis of early development problems.
Age/grade range: Birth through 7 years.
Time to administer: Approximately 1-2 hours for complete test; 10-30 minutes for screening test.

Boehm Test of Basic Concepts–Third Edition (Boehm–3)
by Ann E. Boehm
Published by: The Psychological Corporation/Pearson
Type: Individual or group administration.
What it's used for: To assess students' understanding of basic concepts related to school success.
Age/grade range: Grades K though 2 years.
Time to administer: Approximately 30-45 minutes.

Bracken School Readiness Assessment–Third Edition (Bracken SRA–3)
by Bruce A. Bracken
Published by: The Psychological Corporation/Pearson
Type: Individually administered.
What it's used for: To assess concepts related to school readiness.
Age/grade range: 3 years through 6 years.
Time to administer: Approximately 10-15 minutes.

Metropolitan Readiness Tests, Sixth Edition
by Joanne R. Nurss
Published by: The Psychological Corporation/Pearson
Type: Individual (Level 1) and group administration (Level 2).
What it's used for: To assess literacy in pre-kindergarten and kindergarten
Age/grade range: 4 years to 7 years.
Time to administer: Varies; up to a total of 1 hour-40 minutes in four separate sessions.

Visual-Motor Tests

Bender Visual–Motor Gestalt Test, Second Edition (Bender Gestalt II)
by Gary G. Brannigan & Scott L. Decker
Published by: Riverside Publishing
Type: Individually administered.
What it's used for: To measure visual-motor functioning, such as eye-hand coordination.
Age/grade range: 4 years to adult.
Time to administer: Approximately 10-15 minutes.

Beery-Buktenica Developmental Test of Visual-Motor Integration–6th Edition (Beery VMI)
by Keith E. Beery, Norman A. Buktenica, & Natasha A. Beery
Published by: Pearson
Type: Individual or group administration.
What it's used for: To measure visual-motor functioning, such as eye-hand coordination; visual perception and motor coordination.
Age/grade range: 2 years to adult.
Time to administer: Approximately 10-15 minutes.

Bruininks–Oseretsky Test of Motor Proficiency, Second Edition (BOT–2)
by Robert H. Bruininks & Brett D. Bruininks
Published by: Pearson
Type: Individually administered.
What it's used for: To assess fine and gross motor skills.
Age/grade range: 4 years through 21 years.
Time to administer: Approximately 45-60 minutes

Hooper Visual Organization Test (VOT)
by H. Elston Hooper
Published by: Western Psychological Services
Type: Individually administered.
What it's used for: To assess visual integration; often used as part of neuro-psychological evaluations.
Age/grade range: 5 years and older.
Time to administer: Approximately 15 minutes.

REFERENCES

About the SAT. Retrieved August 22, 2008 from CollegeBoard Web site: http://www.collegeboard.com/student/testing/sat/about.html.

ACT News. (2008). *2008 ACT college readiness report news release.* Retrieved August 22, 2008 from http://www.act.org/news/releases/2008/crr.html.

A decade of effort. (2006, January 5). *Education Week*, pp. 8-16.

American Educational Research Association, American Psychological Association, & National Council on Measurement in Education (1999). *Standards for educational and psychological testing* (Rev. ed.). Washington, D.C.: American Psychological Association.

American Libraries (2005). Interview: Straight answers from Margaret Spellings, *(36)*8, 28.

American Psychological Association. (2004). *Code of fair testing practices.* Washington, DC: Joint Committee on Testing Practices.

American Psychiatric Association. (2000). *Diagnostic and statistical manual of mental disorders(4th ed.), text revision.* Washington, DC: Author.

Associated Press. (1997, June 26). Teachers criticize standardized tests. *Weirton Daily Times*, p. B1.

Black, S. (2005). Acing the exam. *American School Board Journal*, *192*(1), 35-46.

Bolles, R.N. (2010). *What color is your parachute? 2010: A practical manual for job-hunters and career-changers.* Berkeley, CA: Ten Speed Press.

Briggs, D. C. (2004). Evaluating SAT coaching: Gains, effects and self-selection. In R. Zwick (Ed.), *Rethinking the SAT* (pp. 217-233). New York, NY: RoutledgeFalmer.

Briggs, J. (2000). *Fire in the Crucible: Understanding the process of creative genius.* Grand Rapids, MI: Phanes Press.

Butcher, J.N., Perry, J., & Hahn, J. (2004). Computers in clinical assessment: Historical developments, present status, and future challenges. *Journal of Clinical Psychology, 60*(3), 331-345.

Campbell, F.A. & Burchinal, M.R. (2008). Early childhood interventions: In P.C. Kyllonen, R. D. Roberts, & L. Stankov (Eds.), *Extending intelligence: Enhancement and new constructs* (pp. 61-84). New York: Lawrence Erlbaum Associates.

Capps, R., Fix, M., Murray, J., Ost, J., Passel, S., & Herwantoro, S. (2005). The new demography of America's schools: Immigration and the No Child Left Behind Act. The Urban Institute: Washington, D.C.

Cech, S.J. (2007). College-admissions group weights calls to dump SAT. *Education Week, 27*(6), pp. 8-9.

Ceci, S.J., & Williams, W.M. (1997). Schooling, intelligence, and income. *American Psychologist, 52*(11), 1051-1058.

Center on Education Policy (2008, February). Instructional time in elementary schools: A closer look at changes for specific subjects. Downloaded March 26, 2008, from http://www.cep-dc.org/ document/docWindow.cfm?fuseaction=document.viewDocument&documentid=234&documentFormatId=3713.

Cohen, R.J., & Swerdlik, M.E. (2005). *Psychological testing and assessment: An introduction to tests and measurement* (Sixth ed.). Boston: McGraw Hill.

Csikszentmihalyi, M. (1996). Creativity: *Flow and the psychology of discovery and invention.* New York: HarperCollins.

DeAngelis, T. (2010). Successful kids. *Monitor on Psychology, 41*(4), 46-49.

Doll, B. (1996). Prevalence of psychiatric disorders in children and youth: An agenda for advocacy by school psychology. *School Psychology Quarterly, 11,* 20-47.

Dweck, C.S. (2002). Beliefs that make smart people dumb. In R.J. Sternberg (Ed.). *Why smart people can be so stupid.* New Haven: Yale University Press.

Dweck, C.S. (2006). *Mindset: The new psychology of success.* New York: Random House.

Garb, H. N., Wood J. M., Lilienfeld S. O., & Nezworski, M. T. (2002). Effective use of projective techniques in clinical practice: let the data help with selection and interpretation. *Professional Psychology: Research and Practice, 33*(5), 454-463.

Garb, H.N., Klein, D.F., & Grove, W.M. (2002). Comparison of medical and psychological tests. *American Psychologist, 57*(2), 137-138.

Gardner, H. (1983). *Frames of mind: The theory of multiple intelligences.* New York: Basic Books.

Gardner, H. (1994). Cracking open the IQ box. In S. Fraser (Ed.), *The bell curve wars: Race, intelligence, and the future of America.* New York: Basic Books.

Gardner, H. (1999). *Intelligence reframed: Multiple intelligences for the 21st century.* New York: Basic Books.

Gazzaniga, M.S. (2005). *The ethical brain.* New York: Dana Press.

Getting Ready: Findings from the National School Readiness Indicators Initiative: A 17 State Partnership (February 2005). Prepared by Rhode Island KIDS COUNT.

Goe, L. (2007). *The link between teacher quality and student outcomes: A research synthesis.* Washington, DC: National Comprehensive Center for Teacher Quality. Retrieved March 16, 2008 from http://www. ncctq.org/link.php

Goleman, D. (1995). *Emotional intelligence.* New York: Bantam Books.

Goleman, D. (2006). *Social intelligence.* New York: Bantam Books.

Gould, S.J. (1996). *The mismeasure of man.* New York: W.W. Norton.

Greene, H., & Greene, M. (2004, December). Standardized testing: Help or hindrance? *University Business,* 7(12), 25-26.

Herrnstein, R.J., & Murray, C. (1994). *The bell curve: Intelligence and class structure in American life.* New York: Free Press.

Heubert, J.P. (2001). High-stakes testing and civil rights: Standards of appropriate test use and a strategy for enforcing them. In G. Orfield & M.L. Kornhaber (Eds.), *Raising standards or raising barriers? Inequality and high-stakes testing in public education* (pp. 179-194). New York: Century Foundation Press.

Heubert, J.P., & Hauser, R.M. (Eds.) (1999). National Research Council, *High stakes: Testing for tracking, promotion and graduation.* Washington, DC: National Academy Press.

Howe, M.J.A. (1999). *Genius Explained.* Cambridge, UK: Cambridge University Press.

Jaeggi, S.M, Buschkuehl, M., Jonides, J., & Perrig, W.J. (2008). Improving fluid intelligence with training on working memory. *The Proceedings of the National Academy of Sciences USA (PNAS Early Edition).* 1-5. (Obtained May 4, 2008 from www.pnas.org/ cgi/ doi/10.1073/pnas.0801268105.)

Jehlen, A. (Ed.). (2006, April). Rating NCLB: NEA members say it's hurting more than helping. *Neatoday,* 24(7), 24-31.

Jensen, A.R. (1969). How much can we boost IQ and scholastic achievement? *Harvard Educational Review, 39,* 1-123.

Judge Matia's brain camp. (2007, February 24). *The Plain Dealer,* p. B8.

Kluger, J., & Park, A. (2001, April 30). The quest for a superkid. *Time, 157,* 50-55.

Kohn, A. (2002). The dangerous myth of grade inflation. *Chronicle of Higher Education, 49*(11), p. B7.

Kuh, G. D., & Hu, S. (1999). Unraveling the complexity of the increase in college grades from the mid-1980s to the mid-1990s. *Educational Evaluation and Policy Analysis, 21*(3), 297-320.

Leaf, P. J., Alegria, M., Cohen, P., Goodman, S. H., Horwitz, S. M., Hoven, C. W., Narrow, W. E., Vaden-Kiernan, M., & Regier, D. A. (1996). Mental health service use in the community and schools: Results from the four-community MECA Study. Methods for the Epidemiology of Child and Adolescent Mental Disorders Study. *Journal of the American Academy of Child and Adolescent Psychiatry, 35,* 889–897.

Lemov, D. (2010). *Teach like a champion: 49 techniques that put students on the path to college.* San Francisco, CA: Jossey-Bass

Lilienfeld, S. O., Wood J. M., & Garb H. N. (2000). The scientific status of projective techniques. *Psychological Science, 1*(2), 27-66.

McNeil, L. & Valenzuela, A. (2001). The Harmful impact of the TAAS system of testing in Texas: Beneath the accountability rhetoric. In G. Orfield & M.L. Kornhaber (Eds.), *Raising standards or raising barriers? Inequality and high-stakes testing in public education* (pp. 127-150). New York: Century Foundation Press.

Mellon foundation funds three-year study. (2002). Retrieved Feb. 09, 2006, from Mount Holyoke College Web site: http://mtholyoke.edu/offices/comm/sat/mellonsat.shtml.

Nisbett, R. (1994). Race, IQ, and scientism. In S. Fraser (Ed.), *The bell curve wars: Race, intelligence, and the future of America.* New York: Basic Books.

Ordovensky, P. (1997, October 10-12). Putting students to the test. *USA WEEKEND*, pp. 4-5.

Owen, D. & Doerr, M. (1999). *None of the above: The truth behind the SATs.* Lanham, MD: Rowman & Littlefield Publishers, Inc.

Patrick, B.C., Hisley, J., & Kempler, T. (2000). What's everybody so excited about?: The effects of teacher enthusiasm on student intrinsic motivation and vitality. *Journal of Experimental Education, 68*(3), 217-237.

Perkins, D.N. & Grotzer, T.A. (1997). Teaching intelligence. *American Psychologist, 52*(10), 1125-1133.

Perry, K.E., Donohue, K.M., & Weinstein, R.S. (2007). Testing practices and the promotion of achievement and adjustment in first grade. *Journal of School Psychology, 45*(3), 269-292.

Phelps, R. (2003). *Kill the messenger: the war on standardized testing.* New Brunswick, NJ: Transaction Publishers.

Posner, D. (2004). What's wrong with teaching to the test? *Phi Delta Kappan, 85*(10), 749-751.

Reed, E. (2003, March 27). Principals' pink slips tied to poor scores. *The Plain Dealer*, p. B3.

Rose, L. C., & Gallup, A. M. (2005). The 37the annual phi delta kappa/gallup poll of the public's attitudes toward the public schools.. *Phi Delta Kappan, 87*(1), 41-57.

Sackett, P.R., Borneman, M.J., & Connelly, B.S. (2008). High-stakes testing in higher education and employment. *American Psychologist, 63*(4), 215-227.

Sacks, P. (1999). *Standardized minds: The high price of America's testing culture and what we can do to change it.* Cambridge, MA: Perseus Publishing.

Sawyer, R.K. (2006). *Explaining creativity: The science of human innovation.* New York, NY: Oxford University Press.

Schalock, R.L., Borthwick-Duffy, S.A., Bradley, V.J., Buntinx, W.H.E., Coulter, D.L., Craig, E.M.,...Yeager, M.H. (2010). *Intellectual disability: Definition, classification, and systems of supports* (11th ed.). Washington, DC: American Association on Intellectual and Developmental Disabilities.

Sena, J.D.W., Lowe, P.A., & Lee, S.W. (2007). Significant predictors of test anxiety among students with and without learning disabilities. *Journal of Learning Disabilities, 40*(4), 360-376.

Shenk, D. (2010). *The genius in all of us: Why everything you've been told about genetics, talent, and IQ is wrong.* New York: Doubleday.

Society for Personality Assessment. (2005). The status of the Rorschach in clinical and forensic practice: An official statement by the board of trustees of the society for personality assessment. *Journal of Personality Assessment, 85*(2), 219-237.

Solley, B.A. (2007). On standardized testing: An ACEI position paper. *Childhood Education, 84*(1), 31-37.

Stephens, S. (2008, March 7). Do wholesale firings help failing schools? *The Plain Dealer*, p. A1.

Sternberg, R. J. (1985). *Beyond IQ: A triarchic theory of intelligence.* New York: Cambridge University Press.

Sternberg., R. J. (1997). *Successful intelligence: How practical and creative intelligence determine success in life.* New York: Plume.

Sternberg, R.J. (2002, September). The teachers we never forget. *Monitor on Psychology, 33*(8), 68.

Stix, G. (2009, October). Turbocharging the brain. *Scientific American, 301*(4), 46-55.

Testing plus: real accountability with real results. (n.d.). Retrieved Feb. 06, 2006, from National Education Association Web site: http://www.nea.org/accountability/testplus.html.

U.S. Department of Education (2010, March). A blueprint for reform: The reauthorization of the elementary and secondary education act. Retrieved May 9, 2010 from http://www2.ed.gov/policy/elsec/leg/blueprint/blueprint.pdf.

U.S. Department of Education, National Center for Education Statistics. Digest of Education Statistics. Retrieved May 7, 2010 from http://nces.ed.gov/programs/coe/2009/section1/table-cwd-2.asp.

U.S. Department of Education. (2006, Feburary). Overview: No Child Left Behind Is Working. Retrieved March 7, 2006 from http://www.ed.gov/nclb/overview/importance/nclbworking.html.

Viadero, D. (2004). High school course loads tougher, study says. *Education Week, 23*(30), p. 12.

Viadero, D. (2008). Ideas on creative and practical IQ underlie new tests of giftedness. *Education Week, 27*(38), pp. 1, 16.

Williams, J. (2006). Suit filed against high schools' exit exam. AP Headlines. Retrieved Feb. 09, 2006, from http://www.newsday.com/news/nationworld/wire/sns-ap-exit-exam-lawsuit, 0,2340269.story?coll=sns-ap-nationworld-headlines.

INDEX

LaVergne, TN USA
19 December 2010
209377LV00004B/43/P